Life Goes On

A Play

Adrian Hodges

A SAMUEL FRENCH ACTING EDITION

SAMUEL FRENCH

FOUNDED 1830

SAMUELFRENCH-LONDON.CO.UK
SAMUELFRENCH.COM

FOR AMATEUR PRODUCTION ENQUIRIES

UNITED KINGDOM AND WORLD
EXCLUDING NORTH AMERICA
plays@SamuelFrench-London.co.uk
020 7255 4302/01

Each title is subject to availability from Samuel French,

depending upon country of performance.

LIFE GOES ON

First presented at the Haymarket Theatre, Basingstoke, on March 26th, 1997, with the following cast:

George Marlowe	Robert Duncan
Michael Marlowe	Duncan Duff
Debbie Wilson	Caroline Harker
Helen Wilson	Geraldine Alexander
Joyce Marlowe	Serena Evans

Directed by **Daniel Slater**
Designed by **Elroy Ashmore**
Lighting by **David Ripley**

CHARACTERS

George, 42
Michael, 30s
Lucille's Voice, young
Debbie, mid-20s
Helen, 30s
Joyce, 40

The action of the play takes place in the Marlowes' suburban home

Time: the present

AUTHOR'S NOTE

The main set in Act I is the living-room, which can be re-dressed as the bedroom in Act II, Scene 2. Action involving the halls and the stairs can be played at the front of the stage if space is available. Alternatively the bare minimum of props may be used at all times to facilitate scene changes.

AH

ACT I

The main stage is dark. Sombre music plays

A Light comes up slowly on George Marlowe, who was forty-two when he died. Dressed soberly but for a startlingly modern tie that seems out of character with his modest suit, he stares out solemnly into the audience

The music stops abruptly and George's serious expression gives way to a delightfully affable smile

George There was a smashing turnout at the funeral, some faces I hadn't seen for years. People always make a special effort for the big occasion, don't they? The vicar had some wonderful things to say about me, which was kind considering I'd never met him. Of course, the whole thing was more formal than I'd have liked, but that's Joyce for you. I'm very proud of Joyce. She's really taken it on the chin. The whole family has. It's never easy dealing with the unexpected, is it? But, you know, all things considered, I'd say they've all done terribly well.

SCENE 1

The Lights go up on the living-room of the Marlowes' suburban house. About ten o'clock on the night of George Marlowe's funeral

There are a couple of lived-in armchairs, a mismatched office sofa, dining table and drinks cabinet

Michael Marlowe, in his thirties, George's younger brother, handsome and dishevelled, paces the floor restlessly, a cordless phone to his ear. We hear the ringing tone, then a woman's voice at the other end of the line. She has a strong American accent

Lucille's Voice Sylvester Stallone's residence. Lucille speaking.
Michael Is Mr Stallone there? This is Michael Marlowe.

Lucille's Voice Michael who?
Michael (*emphasising it*) Mar-lowe.
Lucille's Voice Oh, sure, Mr Marlowe. How are you today?
Michael Not so good. It's my brother's funeral.
Lucille's Voice (*oblivious*) That's nice.

Pause

I'm afraid Mr Stallone is busy with his personal trainer right now.
Michael Oh... I was wondering if he'd read the script I sent him yet.
Lucille's Voice (*doubtfully*) Which script was that? He's reading a lot
    presently. Was it *Alien Headcrusher*?
Michael No. (*He pauses. Anxiously*) Does he like *Alien Headcrusher*?
Lucille's Voice He thinks it's too subtle.
Michael (*relieved*) My film is called *Rebellion!*
Lucille's Voice Oh, oh, oh, I *adore* that project. I gotta tell you, I *cried*. When
    Duke—what's his name?
Michael Monmouth. The Duke of Monmouth.
Lucille's Voice Right, when Duke Monmouth is about to have his head cut
    off at the end, and he makes that speech about how he may not have made
    it to be king, but he hopes he'll always be king of the people's hearts, well,
    I just ... oh, jeez, it's happening again now ... here I go...

We hear tearful snuffling at the other end of the line

Off the record, Mr Marlowe, I think this project could do for Mr Stallone
what *Braveheart* did for Mel Gibson. It's period with attitude.
Michael (*thrilled*) That's exactly right. (*He pauses*) Do you think he might
    read it soon?
Lucille's Voice I can't promise anything.
Michael Maybe it would help if I set the scene for him a little...?
Lucille's Voice I don't know...
Michael I'd only need a few seconds of his time.
Lucille's Voice (*after a pause*) I'll see if I can connect you.

There is a click as he is put on hold. Michael punches the air

Michael Yes! (*As he waits he wanders over to the cocktail cabinet where he
    gazes at a picture of George and his wife Joyce. He picks it up and stares
    at it sadly for a moment*)

The phone clicks back on

Lucille's Voice Mr Marlowe?

Michael Yes?
Lucille's Voice Mr Stallone can't speak right now. He's doing his sit-ups.
Michael I can wait.
Lucille's Voice I wouldn't recommend it. He does a lot of sit-ups.

Pause

Also, his assistant asked me to tell you we're not sure about the material.
Michael You said you loved it!
Lucille's Voice We just don't go for the ending.
Michael You cried at the ending!
Lucille's Voice Sure ... but the whole beheading thing *is* kind of negative.
Michael Death is very "in" at the moment.
Lucille's Voice Sure, death with an upside.
Michael Upside?
Lucille's Voice You know, *upside*. Like dying to save the world from a rogue asteroid. That's serious upside. We don't have that here.
Michael But that's just entertainment ... this film is art.
Lucille's Voice (*with horror*) Art?
Michael (*desperately*) Look, if I could just speak with Mr Stallone I'm sure I could explain everything...
Lucille's Voice I'm afraid that's not possible right now.
Michael I'll leave my number...
Lucille's Voice (*briskly*) We have your number, Mr Marlowe. I'll see if I can fit you into his schedule. Have a nice day, now.

There is a sharp click as she hangs up

Debbie Wilson enters, carrying two dessert bowls. Debbie, an exceptionally pretty and sweet-natured woman, is in her mid twenties

Michael doesn't see her

Michael Damn! Blast! Sod it and damn it all to hell!
Debbie Oh, Michael.
Michael Debbie! I didn't hear you come in.
Debbie I should have knocked. I suppose you want to be alone. Poor you. I just keep thinking, why George? It's so unfair. I'm not surprised you're angry.
Michael Angry? No, that was about... (*He pauses, looks at the phone and then changes tack quickly*) Well, I just felt I had to let my feelings out somehow.
Debbie I think we all feel like shouting. It's just so ... awful.

Michael Yes. Awful. (*Then, after an uneasy silence*) Warm, isn't it?
Debbie You know what someone said to me at the funeral? "Lovely day for it". As though it was a wedding or a game of cricket.

They lapse into silence. Michael nods at the dessert bowls

Michael Is one of those for me?
Debbie Oh, yes. I thought you might want some jelly and ice-cream.

Michael smiles and takes the bowl, then sits down on the sofa. He stares at the jelly in fascination

Michael That's an astonishing shade of green, isn't it?
Debbie It's lime, I think.
Michael It's positively glowing.
Debbie I gather they put something in to make it look more cheerful.

He stabs at the jelly with his spoon

Michael I hope it hasn't got bits in. I always hated finding lumps of matter in my jelly. I used to pick them out when Mum wasn't looking and load them on to George's plate.
Debbie It's lucky he liked the bits.
Michael I don't think he did, really. He just didn't want me to get into trouble for not eating my fruit. (*He smiles at the memory*)

Debbie gazes at him sympathetically

(*Rallying*) So, what news from the front?
Debbie Helen's still upstairs trying to get Joyce to calm down.
Michael Has she considered calling the fire brigade?
Debbie (*smiling*) You can't blame her for being upset.
Michael A funeral supper and a child's birthday party. How on earth did the caterers manage to mix them up?
Debbie It was the names apparently. George *Marlowe's* funeral supper, but George *Miller's* fifth birthday. (*She pauses*) I thought the guests were very understanding in the circumstances.
Michael They seemed a bit confused by the balloons.

Debbie smiles at him sadly

The odd thing is, Joyce seems more upset about the caterers than about the ... well, about the *reason* for the caterers.

Debbie It's just her way. She's always been like it. She enjoys having something to be angry about. She's like one of those smart bombs you hear so much about these days, sort of floating around innocuously for a while looking for a target, then suddenly locking-on and, boom!

They smile at each other. In the pause that follows Michael shuffles about restlessly, putting cushions behind his back and throwing them away again as he struggles to find a comfortable position on the sofa

You don't look very comfortable on there.

Michael It's terrible. I've never sat on anything like it.

Debbie Oh, I don't think it's intended for actually sitting on.

Michael Of course not. Can't think how I made such a silly mistake.

Debbie It's more for display. It cost thousands originally. Whole herds went into that sofa.

Michael They should have stuffed the original cow. It would have been more comfortable.

Debbie George was terribly proud of it. He always used to say, "it may be uncomfortable, but it's very good quality". (*Her voice breaks. She looks down, her shoulders shaking. She is crying*)

Michael jumps up and rushes over, taking her in his arms

I'm sorry. I'm sorry. It's just so *awful*. He was so sweet, so nice...

Michael Schhh. I know. It's all right.

Debbie What on earth was he doing anyway?

Michael Trying to rewire Joyce's hairdryer.

Debbie I know, but why? He was *hopeless* at anything like that. Machines broke down if he so much as looked at them. He could reduce a perfectly good car to scrap in less than ten minutes under the bonnet. What possessed him to muck about with electricity? It would have been safer to send him swimming with sharks.

Michael You know George. It took him a long time to get going but once he'd decided to do something...

Debbie I don't want to cry. Not when you're being so brave.

Michael holds her tightly, patting her back in a soothing motion and pulling her tightly to him. They hold each other for a few seconds before Michael cautiously moves his hand to a more intimate position. We register the surprise on Debbie's face

Michael?

Michael Yes?

Debbie You've got your hand on my breast.

Michael I know.

Debbie Why?

Michael Well ... because it seems the right place for it. Do you mind?

Debbie In some circumstances I might not. But I'm not sure this is one of them.

Michael Why isn't it?

Debbie Well, for one thing it's the night of your brother's funeral. And for another you're living with my sister.

Michael I wouldn't call what Helen and I are doing "living together" exactly. It's more a kind of armed truce. (*He pauses*) You ought to know it's finished between us.

Debbie I had no idea things were that bad...

Michael Oh, terrible. (*He crosses to the drinks cabinet, offers the whisky bottle to Debbie*)

Debbie shakes her head. He pours himself a generous measure and downs it before refilling the glass

We've grown apart.

Debbie You've always seemed so right for each other. You're both such ... high-flyers.

Michael (*pleased*) I didn't know you saw me as a high-flyer.

Debbie Of course I do. I mean, the closest I ever get to the film industry is looking at the pictures of Jane Seymour's latest wedding in *Hello!* magazine. But you, you're living in it. Parties every night, all that hobnobbing with your celebrity pals...

Michael (*modestly*) There's probably slightly less celebrity hobnobbing than you might imagine.

Debbie I think it's wonderful you've made something of yourself in that world.

Michael Well, I wish Helen shared your good opinion of me.

Debbie You know what Helen's like. She's always been focused on her own career.

Michael Focused? She's *obsessed*. And she's convinced that nobody else's work could possibly be of any importance. (*He pauses*) You can't imagine what it's like living with someone who has no faith in you. She has this idea that being a film producer is some kind of cakewalk, and it's not, you know. It's *tough*; it may look glamorous, but, my God, we're talking kill or be killed, law of the jungle, vicious, bloody hand-to-hand combat *every day*.

Debbie You make it sound like trench warfare.

Michael (*passionately*) That's what it feels like! But I think I've done all right. I think I deserve a little respect.

Debbie (*carefully*) Perhaps Helen would be more sympathetic if you'd actually ... *made* something.

Michael (*explosively*) That's exactly the kind of nit-picking attitude I always get from her! These things take time, you know! There's a lot of ... preparation involved.

Debbie I'm sure there is.

Michael You have no idea of the technicalities.

Debbie (*chastened*) No. Of course I haven't. (*She goes to him anxiously*) I'm sorry, Michael, I didn't mean to upset you. I think you're wonderful and very talented.

Michael You're only saying that.

Debbie No, I mean it. Really.

Michael (*moving closer*) At least you understand me.

Pause

You know, you're very beautiful.

Debbie Michael...

Michael I mean it. You are. Look, I know I shouldn't have touched your breast before but I've been feeling so rotten about George, and you were there looking so sweet and kind and lovely, and it just sort of happened.

Pause

Can I do it again?

Debbie (*after a moment*) All right. If you want to.

He does. He kisses her. They hold each other tentatively

The door opens and Helen walks in. She is in her thirties, attractive, dressed in impeccable designer mourning clothes

Helen What on earth are you two doing?

They spring apart guiltily

Michael Comforting each other.

Helen It looked like you were...

Michael What?

Helen Well ... it looked a bit more than comforting to me.

Michael That's ridiculous. You're being paranoid.

Helen I'm far from paranoid, Michael. Two years in therapy have proved that, if nothing else.

Michael How's it going, by the way? Any breakthroughs?

Helen Don't change the subject.

Michael For God's sake, Hel, she's your sister ... we're virtually family...
I mean, come on ... you don't *really* think...

Helen (*after a moment*) It just looked as though... (*She pauses*) Look, sorry,
I probably jumped to the wrong conclusion. I'm on edge.

Michael We all are. How's Joyce?

Helen About as well as can be expected. It hasn't been easy for her. We've
all got to do what we can to help.

Debbie I keep offering but she won't let me do anything.

Helen She's trying to keep herself busy. Things were bad enough as it was
without the catering fiasco.

Michael Still, look on the bright side. At least we cancelled the clown in time.

Helen glares at him. Debbie steps in quickly

Debbie The funeral itself went well though, didn't it?

Helen Yes. It was a nice service. George would have liked it.

Michael If it hadn't been his.

Helen The vicar said some lovely things about him, didn't he?

Michael I suppose giving everyone a rousing send-off is in the job
description. I mean, when was the last time you heard a vicar stand up and
say, actually, so-and-so was a lousy husband, a terrible father, contributed
absolutely sod all to the sum of human happiness and we're all glad to see
the back of him?

Helen I think you ought to stop drinking.

Michael I can hold my drink perfectly well, thank you.

Helen I don't want any scenes tonight. We have to think of Joyce. (*She takes
out her mobile and tries to dial but finds the battery is flat*) Damn. (*She
tosses it on the sofa and picks up the main phone*)

Michael turns on her in alarm

Michael I'd rather you didn't use that.

Helen Why on earth not?

Michael People might be trying to get through with messages of condolence.

Helen They'll phone back. The markets were horribly volatile this morning.
I don't want to get caught out. (*She picks up the phone again*)

Michael takes it from her hand

Michael Look, I'm expecting a call.

Helen Michael, it's vital I keep an eye on things. This whole business with
George couldn't have come at a worse time for me.

Michael The timing wasn't that great for him, either.

Helen You know what I mean. I'm under an enormous amount of pressure just now.

Michael The monetary system isn't going to go into free fall just because you miss one day at the office, Helen.

Helen (*with biting sarcasm*) I had no idea you'd become such an expert all of a sudden.

Michael All right, point taken——

Helen (*steaming into him*) I've got a hundred million dollars hanging out there invested in equities and convertible bonds. If I take my eyes off that money for one second, if I don't keep moving it around the markets in search of a safe haven, it could halve in value in a few hours, with the net result that the bank will have some very unhappy clients and yours truly will be out on the street.

Michael For God's sake, Helen, nobody's going to think worse of you for attending your brother-in-law's funeral.

Helen Oh, everyone's considerate enough on the surface, but believe me, underneath they're just waiting for the slightest opportunity to stab you in the back.

Michael You should know. You've wielded the knife often enough.

Helen Thank you so for your support.

Pause

At least I'm prepared to go out and *work* for a living.

Michael I didn't think it would be long before we got round to that.

Helen I mean, I quite fancy being a "film producer" too, if all it involves is rolling out of bed at eleven, making a few phone calls and then getting legless in some ghastly club for the rest of the day with people who shave their heads and dress like a collection of gargoyles.

Michael There's no point getting up early. Los Angeles isn't on line until five.

Helen (*laughing mirthlessly*) You know, I'd prefer it if you were just an honest layabout. It's the self-delusion I can't stand, this endless fantasy that everything is just about to fall into place.

Michael As a matter of fact it is.

Helen (*to Debbie*) You see? It's pathological.

Michael And that's exactly why I don't want you to use the phone.

Helen Who precisely are you expecting to hear from this time?

Michael I can't tell you. Negotiations are at a very delicate stage.

Helen I've had enough of this. Give me that phone.

Michael No.

Debbie Stop it, you two. Please.

Helen I said, give me that phone.

Michael folds his arms stubbornly

Right. (*She tries to grab the phone*)

He holds it up in the air beyond her reach. She stamps hard on his foot. He grimaces in pain but hangs on grimly

Debbie (*shouting*) Stop it!

They turn to her in surprise

For heaven's sake, George is dead! Neither of you should be thinking about work now.

Michael He *was* my brother, Debbie, and I promise you he wouldn't want us all sitting around being miserable on his account. He'd expect us to get on with things.

Debbie You're only saying that because it suits you.

Helen Michael's got a point, Debbie—for once. George was never one to draw attention to himself.

Michael It's not that I'm not upset. I just know George was a big supporter of my film and he'd want me to seize every opportunity to make it happen.

Debbie (*furious with him*) You know what, Michael? I'm sorry I let you kiss me now.

Helen Pardon?

Joyce enters with a tray loaded with tea things. She is forty, and in some ways the most handsome of a good-looking trio of sisters, though her conventional dress and brusque manner tends to obscure this. She puts the tray on the coffee table

Joyce I've been thinking about sleeping arrangements.

Helen Apparently you're not the only one.

Joyce Have I missed something?

Helen Debbie was just saying something about kissing——

Michael (*cutting in desperately*) Let me help you with that, Joyce.

Joyce I can manage. (*She pauses*) Kissing? Whatever for?

Michael That's a marvellous tea set, Joyce.

Joyce It's Royal Doulton.

Michael I always think tea has just that extra bit of flavour in a bone china cup. Is it new?

Joyce Good heavens, no. It was a wedding present.

Pause. They all look at her with concern. She colours but recovers quickly, her manner a touch manic

Who was it from, now? Great Aunt Mary, I think. No, I tell a lie, it was Daddy's cousin Violet. You knew Violet, didn't you, Helen? Big woman, inordinately proud of that ghastly artificial leg of hers. Always used to take it off and pass it round the table after Christmas dinner. (*She pauses. A bit lost*) Sorry, what was it you were saying, Debbie?

Debbie It doesn't matter.

Joyce Well, it'll keep, I expect. (*She pauses*) Now, where was I? Oh, yes, beds. There's only the one double so obviously you and Michael should sleep in the main bedroom tonight, Helen.

Helen But what about you?

Joyce Oh, I'll be perfectly all right in the guest room.

Helen We can't possibly take your room, Joyce, not tonight. It wouldn't feel right. That bed belongs to you and...

George's name hangs heavily in the air. Joyce moves briskly to change the sudden awkward mood

Joyce You know how narrow the one in the guest room is. Two together in that would be like playing Sardines.

Michael Don't worry, I'll take the sofa.

Joyce Are you sure? Well, it's very thoughtful of you... Debbie, you can manage on the camp bed in the small bedroom. (*She stares at the tea things vaguely, suddenly looking lost*)

Helen Are you all right, Joycie?

Joyce Of course I'm all right. You don't have to keep asking.

Pause

I should have catered the day myself. I can see that now. It's always risky leaving these things in the hands of strangers. But you don't expect people to make a mess of such a simple task, do you?

They look at her sympathetically

Still, there's no point blaming anyone else. It's entirely my own fault.

Helen How can it possibly be your fault?

Joyce I should have anticipated it. It's just the kind of thing that *would* happen to my husband. Only George Marlowe could manage to turn his own funeral into low farce.

Michael It's not as though he had much say in the catering.

Helen (*glancing angrily at Michael*) For Heaven's sake, Joyce. These things just … happen.

Joyce You can say that, but the fact is it's absolutely typical. George couldn't even get himself buried without finding one last way to embarrass me.

Helen Look, are you *sure* you're all right?

Joyce I'm absolutely fine.

Helen Only, if you weren't, and you want to talk to someone, I can give you the name of a very good man.

Joyce What are you talking about?

Michael A shrink.

Joyce Helen, have I *ever* struck you as the kind of person who might turn to a complete stranger for advice during a crisis?

Helen It's just that you seem so——

Joyce (*cutting in*) All I'm doing is trying to get through this whole thing in a reasonably dignified way. I dare say your precious head doctors would prefer me to be weeping and wailing and *getting it all out in the open*, or whatever the modish phrase is for drawing attention to oneself, but I'm sorry, I can't. I'm just not made that way.

Pause

Debbie (*quietly*) It's just that you sound so angry with George.

Joyce This isn't anger, Debbie, it's honesty. The simple truth is that he was a man who attracted disaster like a magnet. I'm sorry, but that's the way it was, and now he's dead I'm certainly not going to sentimentalise his memory. (*She pauses. With sudden venom*) Michael, why are you cuddling that phone?

Michael looks suspiciously at Helen

Michael I'm expecting a call.

Joyce Hugging the thing doesn't make it any more likely to ring.

Michael meekly puts the phone down on the coffee table

Debbie I don't think George was a failure at all.

Joyce You didn't have to live with him.

Pause

Other people are allergic to cats or penicillin. With George it was money.

Debbie Money isn't everything.

Joyce People often say that, but hardly ever when they need it.

Pause

I've been sitting here these past few days since ... it happened ... wondering if George was actually good at anything at all. Work? Never got off the bottom rung of the ladder... Sport? Hopeless. The hand to eye coordination of a six month old baby...

Michael Monopoly.

Joyce What?

Michael He had an extraordinary flair for Monopoly. I put countless hotels on Park Lane and Mayfair, and he never landed on them once.

Debbie (*after a moment*) He was the kindest man I ever met.

Joyce What?

Debbie (*fiercely*) I said, he was the kindest man I ever met.

Joyce Oh, kindness is easy. Kindness butters no parsnips.

Debbie I don't understand why you're being so hard on him.

Michael I thought it was "fine words".

Joyce Fine words? What are you talking about?

Michael That don't butter parsnips.

Joyce It was always "kindness" in our family.

Michael No, I'm sure it's "fine words".

Helen For God's sake, Michael, do you really think anyone cares?

Debbie (*close to tears*) I know you're upset, Joyce, but I just can't listen to you talking like this about George any more. I think he was a lovely man, and I think kindness *does* matter.

Debbie goes out, closing the door with a bang

There is a moment of silence

Joyce Well. I suppose we might have expected that little scene. It must stem from being the youngest. I suspect she's always known she was an unplanned pregnancy.

Michael You were over-doing it a bit, Joyce.

Joyce I don't think so.

Michael He was my brother, you know. And I think you *were*. I better see if Debbie's all right.

Michael goes out, avoiding a searching glare from Helen

The Lights go down in the living-room and up in the hall

Debbie sits miserably at the bottom of the stairs

Have you got room on that step?

Debbie No, as it happens.

Michael I don't blame you for being angry with me.

Debbie You told me it was all over between you and Helen.

Michael It is. (*He pauses*) As good as.

Debbie Were you planning to let her know?

Michael I've been waiting for the right moment. (*He pauses*) This didn't seem the right time to confront it. (*He pauses*) I can see how it all might have looked.

Debbie I'll tell you how it looked. It looked like a man with a live-in partner who fancied a bit on the side. I really do like you, Michael, but I don't like hypocrites and liars.

Michael Supposing I cut back on lying and concentrated on hypocrisy?

Debbie I'm not joking. (*She pauses. Strongly*) I wasn't thinking straight when you kissed me before. (*She pauses*) You *did* at least mean what you said about feeling awful, didn't you?

Michael Of course.

Debbie Everyone seems to have forgotten why we're here. Joyce is so angry, Helen can't stop thinking about the City, and you... I mean, how can you worry about a *film* so much with George suddenly ... gone...?

Michael I don't know what else to do.

Debbie What?

Michael I don't know what to do except ... carry on. Objectively I know George is dead but *subjectively* it doesn't have any meaning. I don't *feel* it. Nothing seems any different.

Debbie Denial.

Michael What?

Debbie You're in denial.

Michael (*emphatically*) No, I'm not.

They both smile at his feeble joke

Look, it may be terrible but the thing that seems more real to me right now is that if I can just persuade a very well known actor to be in my film then I'll definitely be able to raise the money to make it. And if that sounds selfish, then... (*He shrugs helplessly*)

Debbie Didn't you like George?

Michael Of course I did. I mean, most of what Joyce said about him is true I suppose, but that's *why* I like him.

Debbie Liked.

Michael Sorry?

Debbie Liked. You said "like". Present tense.

Michael Did I?

Debbie (*after a moment*) I suppose I *do* understand what you're saying about your film. And you're right about one thing. George wouldn't want you to miss your chance.

Michael (*looking at her intently*) I meant everything I said before, Debbie. I really do think you're beautiful.

Debbie Michael! I'm not... I mean, I suppose my legs are all right, but my eyes are too far apart and I've got a big bum. (*She pauses*) But it's nice of you to say it.

Michael I *am* going to get the situation with Helen sorted out. I just wanted the funeral over with first. (*He pauses*) You do like me, don't you?

Debbie (*simply*) I love you. I always have. Ever since I was a schoolgirl.

Michael Oh. (*He pauses*) That sounds good.

Debbie It *wasn't* good, it was horrible. You never noticed me at all and then Helen got hold of you, so I had to sit there every Christmas and birthday watching you touching each other in that casual, exclusive way that lovers do, laughing at private jokes and going off into corners together and ... *kissing*. I was insanely jealous.

Michael I had no idea.

Debbie And the worst, most stupid thing is I've never really got over it. (*She pauses*) Which is probably the very last thing I should tell you.

Michael Oh, I can think of worse.

Debbie So I suppose what I'm saying is, if you still want me, you can have me.

A grin of delighted anticipation spreads slowly across Michael's face

There is one thing though. Everything's been so strange these last few days, and ... well, what I mean is, you wouldn't try to take advantage of the situation, would you?

Michael Of course not!

Debbie You really do want to be with me? For more than just sex?

Michael Debbie, I promise you, sex is almost the last thing on my mind...

Debbie Only, a man who took advantage of his brother's death to seduce his girlfriend's sister when she was emotionally vulnerable for nothing more than a quick roll in the hay ... well, I think I could *hate* a man who did something like that.

Michael Could you?

Debbie I'm pretty sure I *would*. (*She pauses*) That's not what you're doing, is it?

Michael Of course not. (*He pauses*) I love you.

Debbie is visibly affected by this. We hear the phone ringing, off

(*Looking up; distractedly*) So, if I understand you correctly ... what you're saying is ... it would be all right if I came to see you later on?

Debbie Tonight might be a bit awkward.
Michael I'll be very quiet.
Debbie I tend to be quite noisy.
Michael I meant, getting there.
Debbie (*grinning*) So did I.
Michael (*startled and pleased by the innuendo*) I'll wait until everyone's asleep.
Debbie All right, then.
Michael You are sure it's what you want?

She nods. Michael can hardly believe his good fortune

The Lights go down on the hall and up on the living-room. Helen and Joyce are as they were when Michael and Debbie went out

Helen It's completely unnecessary for Michael to go rushing after her like that.
Joyce He's only being considerate.
Helen The pair of them have been behaving oddly all night.
Joyce I haven't noticed anything.
Helen They're up to something.
Joyce I'm sure that's not true.
Helen Debbie said, quite distinctly, that she was sorry she'd kissed him.
Joyce Then you're misinterpreting things, as always.
Helen "As always"? What does that mean?
Joyce You've got an over-active imagination. Mother always said so.
Helen Well, she was wrong!
Joyce And you're chronically insecure.
Helen (*grinding it out*) I am not being insecure.
Joyce Your suspicious nature has ruined a string of promising relationships.
Helen That's completely untrue. Name one relationship that failed because of me.
Joyce All right... Graham.
Helen Graham? Graham! He was gay!
Joyce Not until afterwards. (*She pauses*) What about Dennis?
Helen Oh, for God's sake, Joyce, Dennis was married.
Joyce I can see I'm going to be shouted down no matter what.

Pause

But I will say this. There's only one person in this family who's ever felt the need to consult a *psychiatrist*.
Helen *Analyst* to be precise.

Joyce It's all the same pseudo-scientific claptrap.

Helen Joyce, why is it you always reserve your strongest opinions for things you know nothing whatsoever about?

Joyce It doesn't matter how many insults you hurl at me, Helen. We both know what I'm talking about.

Helen (*controlling herself with a huge effort*) All I said was, there is something odd going on between Michael and Debbie.

Joyce And I'm telling you you've made a mistake.

Helen I don't know why you're getting so excited about it.

Joyce I just think it's a cruel thing to say when it's untrue.

Helen Let's leave it, shall we?

Joyce Fine.

The phone rings. Joyce picks it up furiously

Hello?

Lucille's Voice Hi, I'm ringing for Mr Stallone...

Joyce (*not listening*) What? Stone?

Lucille's Voice No, Stallone. My name is Lucille. We have a proposal to make——

Joyce (*cutting across her*) A proposal? Good God, don't you people ever go to bed?

Lucille's Voice I only just got up!

Joyce I have no interest whatsoever in anything you have to sell me. The last thing I need at this precise moment is a lecture on the virtues of double-glazing.

Lucille's Voice Double glazing?

Joyce And the name is Marlowe by the way, not Stone. Thank you so much. Goodbye. (*She clicks the receiver off irritably*)

Helen Who was it?

Joyce Some halfwit saleswoman.

Helen shakes her head, then walks to the door

Where are you going?

Helen My car.

Joyce What on earth for?

Helen My mobile's dead. As Michael seems intent on monopolising the phone in here I'll have to charge it from the engine.

Joyce The City can't possibly still be working at this time.

Helen London may be asleep, Joyce, but Tokyo is very much awake.

She opens the door just as Michael comes in

Helen glares at him but goes out without comment

He looks after her anxiously

Michael (*to Joyce*) Anything wrong?

Joyce She's convinced that Japan's economy will collapse without her personal intervention.

Michael Was that the phone I heard?

Joyce What? Oh, yes. Nuisance caller, windows, kitchens or some such. (*She pauses*) Helen said something odd a moment ago.

Michael That's not completely unprecedented.

Joyce She thought there might be something going on between you and Debbie.

Michael How ridiculous.

Joyce That's what I said.

Michael I don't know where she gets these ideas. Can I have another drink?

Joyce Help yourself. So, there isn't anything?

Michael Hmmmm?

Joyce Between you and Debbie?

Michael Good Lord, no. (*He pours his drink with studied casualness*)

Joyce stands very near to him. He turns, startled to find her so close

Joyce Don't you have something to say to me, Michael?

Michael Well ... ummm... I'm terribly sorry about George of course ... but...

Joyce Nothing else?

Michael (*stumped*) Would you like a drink?

Joyce No, thank you. (*She looks at him meaningfully*)

Michael is bewildered

Michael You wouldn't like to give me a clue, would you?

Joyce If you're worrying about the ... appropriateness ... you have my full permission to say what's on your mind.

Michael (*helplessly*) Thank you, Joyce ... it's just that I can't quite think...

Joyce misinterprets his confusion as disapproval. She turns away, flustered

Joyce I'm sorry, Michael, you're quite right. This is neither the time nor the place. (*She pauses*) I think it's time I went to bed. Today's all been a bit too much for me. (*She pauses. Briskly*) You'll find sheets and blankets in the drawer on the landing. (*She gives him a last lingering look before walking to the door*)

He stares after her, struggling for some explanation for her behaviour

Michael Joyce? I haven't done something terrible, have I?
Joyce Not in my opinion.
Michael Only, if I have, whatever it is, I'm sorry.
Joyce We're both mature adults, Michael. Neither of us has anything to apologise for.

Joyce goes out

Michael, perplexed and swaying slightly, replenishes his glass from the near-empty whisky bottle. He does not realize how drunk he is. Suddenly, the Lights begin to go up, gradually at first, then until they are unnaturally bright. Michael pauses with his glass to his lips

Michael Hello. (*He walks to the light switch and clicks it off*)

Nothing happens. He jiggles the switch up and down but the Lights remain unaffected. A moment, then all at once they reach a peak of intensity, then snap off, plunging the stage into darkness

George Michael?
Michael What? Who said that?

The Lights go up to reveal that George is now standing across the room from Michael, wearing the same suit and loud tie as in his first scene

Michael stares at him in utter disbelief. Hold on them for a moment before the Lights go down abruptly

SCENE 2

The Friday before Scene 1, 7 p.m.

Darkness, then the Lights come up on George at the edge of the stage, dressed as before

George Of course, Joyce is absolutely right. The whole thing really is all my fault. I don't blame her for being angry. (*He pauses*) It's just that there are moments in a marriage when you realize that you've lost the capacity to *surprise* your partner. You have this image of each other that can't be changed. Well, I thought it was time to prove that I *could* change. I wanted to surprise her. (*He pauses*) Which, if you think about it, I suppose I did.

The Lights go down on George and up in the living-room—evening sunshine outside

Joyce is peering through the net curtains. She curses under her breath

Joyce It's still there. Damn the man. (*She pauses and shouts*) George? George!

George (*off*) Yes, darling?

Joyce It's still there.

George (*off*) Sorry?

Joyce It's sheer provocation.

George (*off*) It is the public highway, Joycie.

Joyce Why doesn't he park in front of his own house? And why in God's name does he need a four wheel drive around here anyway? It's not as though Croydon has many mountain ranges.

George enters, in slippers, baggy trousers and jumper, carrying a newspaper

George They like to get out and about at weekends. The Lake District, that kind of thing.

Joyce You've spoken to him?

George Oh, yes. We had quite a nice chat.

Joyce And?

George And what?

Joyce What did he *say*?

George That Windermere is marvellous in the autumn.

Joyce (*controlling herself*) I mean, what did he say about parking that bloody tank outside my front window every night?

George Oh, I'm not sure the subject really came up.

Joyce You're not sure?

George Well ... it didn't.

Joyce I specifically told you to speak to him about it.

George I suppose I must have forgotten. (*He pauses*) I'm sure you'd like him if you met him——

Joyce The space in front of our house should be reserved for our car. I'm sick of parking halfway back to the M25.

George There's no rule that says we own the space, dear——

Joyce What about the rule of common decency? I swear, if I make one more trip to Sainsbury's and find that ... thing there when I come back, I won't be responsible for my actions.

George laughs amiably at this. Joyce looks at him in disbelief

Did I say something funny?

George (*going to the armchair*) You've always made me laugh, Joycie. The way your mind works.

Joyce You needn't think you can sit down. There's far too much to do. Michael and Helen will be here in an hour and I haven't even got the potatoes on yet.

George Just ten minutes with the *Evening Standard* and I'll be at your beck and call. (*He pauses*) "Beck and call". "*Beck* and call". Must be the noun form of *beckon*. Beck. Pretty archaic now. Don't often summon someone with a *beck* these days, do we?

Joyce Have you finished?

George Pardon?

Joyce Do you really think I've got time to stand here listening to you chewing the cud over some arcane proverb?

George Oh, I don't think it's a proverb, more a saying...

He sees the look on her face

Just an observation...

His voice trails off at her warning look

I know what this is all about. It's the fence, isn't it?

Joyce It's not just the fence.

George I promise I'll do it next weekend. You'll be astonished by that fence, Joyce. It will *shine*. People will flock from miles around to see it. The Great Wall of China will be dead as a tourist attraction overnight.

Joyce There's no need to be sarcastic.

George I just wanted you to be proud of the fence.

Joyce You haven't painted it yet.

George But I'm going to. Next weekend. (*He pauses*) Or the one after at the very latest.

Joyce You see, you're putting it off already.

George Well, be fair, Joycie, I have to read up on the whole subject. You can't just pick up a can of paint and slap it on. It takes a bit of thinking about.

Joyce Two undercoats and a gloss finish. How much thinking can it possibly need?

George You see? The traps are already opening up in front of you. I would have thought matt was the thing for a fence.

Joyce Good God, George, matt, gloss, what's the difference?

George Could be all the difference in the world. Don't worry, I'll look into it. They've got a book on paint in the library. I noticed it the last time I was in the letter P.

Joyce stares at him, riled by his placidity

Joyce What is it you *do* down at that library hour after hour, anyway?
George Oh, nothing much.
Joyce You just sit there and ... *read* all day?
George That's about the size of it.
Joyce If we were talking about anyone else I'd think it was a mistress.
George I don't see why you assume that's so unlikely.
Joyce I would have thought it was fairly obvious.
George I've had offers, you know.
Joyce (*startled*) Who from?
George It would be ungallant of me to say.
Joyce Not that dumpy little woman from the Dry Cleaners?
George I wouldn't say dumpy. I'd call her petite.
Joyce I've seen thinner barrage balloons. *Was* it her?
George No, as it happens.
Joyce Who then?
George Oh, I couldn't possibly say.
Joyce You can't because you're making it up.
George I certainly am not.
Joyce This is utter nonsense. I don't want to talk about it any more.
George You started it.
Joyce All I did was ask why you spend so much time in the library. The next thing I know you're flaunting your other women at me.
George I was simply making the point that despite your oft-stated view to the contrary, there are one or two other women in the hemisphere who find me sexually attractive.

This reduces Joyce to silence for a moment. When she speaks again her manner is slightly more muted

Joyce Well, what do you say to this army of groupies, then?
George I tell them there's only ever been one woman for me. (*He smiles at her affectionately*)

She tries to look angry but can't help but be mollified

Why don't you come over here and kiss me?
Joyce I can't do that. There simply isn't time.
George No time for even one kiss?
Joyce It's not the kiss as such. It's the whole thinking behind the kiss. I've made *plans* for this evening and I can't afford to have them thrown into disarray. You always think that some absurd compliment or romantic gesture is going to make everything all right. Well, it doesn't. A kiss doesn't paint the fence, does it?

George I suppose not.

Joyce This house is falling apart. The roof is leaking. The grouting on the bathroom tiles needs renewing. The guttering has collapsed. The lino is coming up in the kitchen...

George I think the old place is comfortable enough. It looks homely to me.

Joyce ...And, as I've mentioned to you on numerous occasions, my hairdryer is playing up. There's a loose connection somewhere. Drying my hair is an absolute nightmare.

George You know I'm not very good with that kind of thing, Joycie.

Joyce I wouldn't mind if we could pay someone to do all these jobs.

George When my promotion comes through you can have all the handymen you want.

Joyce They've been promising you that promotion for years. The fact is you've been shabbily treated by the Civil Service and you're too soft to confront them about it. The only thing you've ever got from your job is this ridiculous sofa.

George It was a terrific bargain.

Joyce George, they were replacing all the furniture. They'd have given it to you for nothing.

George With respect, darling, you don't understand the Civil Service mentality. They never give anything away. They'd rather burn it.

Joyce I don't know why you were so mad keen on it anyway.

George I think it looks very grand.

Joyce But it doesn't match anything. It has "office" written all over it. (*Her attention is distracted by something outside the window*) He's going!

George What?

Joyce Your pal with the HGV. Well, go on, get the car before the space disappears.

George We're only just down the road——

Joyce George, get the car!

George knows an order when he hears one. He gets up wearily and goes out

Joyce watches through the window. We hear the sound of car engines off, then the sudden squealing of brakes

A moment, then George reappears in the doorway, looking hangdog

(*After a long, cold pause*) You sat there and let her park in front of you.

George I never even saw her coming. It's that left turn. You can nip straight in.

Joyce You *waved* her on.

George It may have looked like a wave. If you'd been closer you'd have seen I was actually shaking my fist.

Joyce It's outrageous. First we have to contend with that bus of his, now it's the little woman's runaround as well. There's only one thing for it. We'll have to put cones out every time we leave.

George I don't think that's legal.

Joyce The legality of it holds no fascination for me whatever. This is a war, George, pure and simple. And, despite your feeble attempts at appeasement, I do not intend to be the loser.

Joyce goes out

George sits down with a sigh. He tries to interest himself in the newspaper, without success

He looks up to find Michael in the doorway, grinning

George Mike!
Michael The door was open.
George Come in, come in.

Michael is clutching a bottle of champagne and a tatty-looking bunch of flowers. He looks dishevelled in a leather jacket, jeans and loose shirt. He is drunk

Michael (*holding up the bottle*) Champagne.
George Wonderful. Special occasion?
Michael My film is as good as there.
George That's marvellous news.
Michael Just a question of dotting the Ts and crossing the Is. (*He pauses. He thinks*) Did I get that right?
George Very nearly.
Michael I'm a bit pissed. I've been celebrating.
George I can't say I blame you. When's it starting then?
Michael Oh, soon. It's just a matter of setting the date now.
George Make sure we get invited to the premiere, won't you?
Michael Best seats in the house, guaranteed. How are you both?
George Oh, mustn't complain. I've upset Joyce a bit, I'm afraid.
Michael Easy to do.
George Oh, I don't know. She's pretty good most of the time. She worries too much. That's my fault I expect.
Michael It's probably stress.
George Stress?

Michael I read somewhere we're all suffering from it. Heart attacks, cancer, ulcers, colds, flu, verrucas, all down to stress.

George Sounds convincing.

Michael If you could get Joyce to purge the stress from her life she'd be as calm as a Tibetan monk.

George Serene.

Michael That's the word.

George She used to be serene, you know.

Michael No offence, but I can't really imagine it.

George You didn't see us so much in the early days. It was different then.

Michael Was it?

George Not that she was ever Mary Poppins, exactly. Come to think of it, she assaulted the waiter at my favourite restaurant during our very first date. The soup was cold, I think. I mean, I didn't want to make a fuss, but good old Joycie, she was right in there with the verbal machete.

Michael Didn't it put you off her a bit?

George God, no. I loved it. I thought, this is a woman who knows her own mind and isn't afraid to say it. Fantastic. And, of course, to coin a phrase, she's very beautiful when she's angry.

Michael That must be why she's angry all the time then. Some kind of beauty treatment.

George (*smiling, not minding the jibe*) I think I've disappointed her somewhere along the line, you know, Mike. (*He pauses. With genuine puzzlement*) I've always done my best, but it never seems to be quite enough.

Joyce enters in her apron. She stops in surprise

Michael kisses her

Joyce (*to George*) Why didn't you tell me Michael was here?

Michael Hello, Joyce. (*He offers her the flowers*) They're a bit wilted, I'm afraid.

Joyce They just need a drop of water.

George Nothing short of a trip to Lourdes is going to revive those flowers.

Joyce (*fiercely*) It's the thought that counts. (*She pauses*) Look at me. I'm a mess. Drinks? What about drinks?

George I was just about to offer when you came in.

Michael (*handing her the champagne*) I brought you this. Sorry, it got a bit warm *en route*.

Joyce Champagne!

Michael Well, very nearly.

Joyce (*looking at the label*) I had no idea they were making it in Rumania these days.

Michael I read about it in one of the Sunday supplements. It's produced just outside Bucharest in a co-op run entirely by former secret policemen. The wine critic said he'd never tasted anything like it.

Joyce I'm sure it'll be lovely. I'll put it on ice for a minute. (*She pauses. Agitated*) You've taken us completely by surprise, Michael. We weren't expecting you for an hour yet. The food's only just on. I'm not even changed.

Michael I'll nip down the pub for a few minutes if you like.

Joyce Don't be silly.

George Mike's celebrating. His film starts shooting any minute.

Michael Everyone loves the script. All we need to do now is persuade a star name to be in it and we're up and running.

George I thought you said you were going to use a cast of young unknown actors?

Michael Oh, we are, by and large. We just need someone famous for one or two of the bigger parts. But it'll be done with complete integrity.

Joyce Remind me what the film's about.

Michael The Monmouth rebellion. The story's got everything. The Duke of Monmouth is a gentle scholar with a distant claim to the throne. He resists all overtures to take up arms against the corrupt regime of King James. Then the woman he loves is killed protecting her pet deer by the King's personal bodyguard during a hunting trip. Mad with grief, Monmouth abandons his books and cuts the man to pieces in a duel. He finds the whole West Country rising in his support. Before he knows it all Devon is on fire. He realizes that his destiny is to lead his people against the tyrant. It's *El Cid* meets Quentin Tarantino.

George And it's all true, is it?

Michael It's true to the *spirit* of the way things happened.

George They cut his head off in the end, didn't they?

Michael Yes.

George Personally I've always preferred a happy ending.

Michael (*working himself up*) Oh, well, fine, yes, *of course* it should have a happy ending. I mean, who wants all those depressing tragedies? Why ever didn't Shakespeare remind Juliet to pack her alarm clock? And what a pity Tolstoy forgot to save Anna Karenina with a last minute decision to re-route the train arriving at platform five from Moscow to Minsk!

George Well, of course, when you put it that way...

Michael Some stories just don't have happy endings, George. That's life.

Joyce Of course it is. I really think you could be a little more supportive, George. After all, Michael's worked awfully hard for this opportunity.

George I'm sorry, Mike. Don't take any notice of me at all.

Joyce (*looking around*) For heaven's sake, George, you haven't even put the snacks out yet. Poor Michael must be starving.

George Sorry. Forgot.

Joyce goes out with the flowers

George goes to the cabinet and emerges with crisps

Have you tried these? Garlic and Mint flavour Gourmet Potato Slices, handmade from only the finest young Swedish potatoes. Amazing. Have you visited the snack section in the supermarket lately? You could spend *days* browsing on that aisle. It's all gone way beyond the traditional tussle between salt'n'vinegar and cheese and onion. (*He pauses*) Oven baked, deep-fried, shallow-fried, grilled, steamed, thin cut, medium cut, thick cut, crinkle cut, high-fat, no fat, low in sodium, high in polyunsaturates; and *every* flavour under the sun. I mean, say what you like about seventeen years of Conservative government but they promised us freedom of choice and, by God, when it came to nibbles they certainly delivered.

Michael I'm a bit of a Twiglet man myself.

George Oh, I agree. No need for any fashionable modifications there. You know where you are with a Twiglet.

Joyce enters with Michael's flowers in a small vase. They are a dismal sight

Joyce Plenty of life in those yet.

They contemplate the sad brown stalks without conviction. Joyce bustles about with the champagne and an ice bucket

This won't take a moment to cool down. What about something while we're waiting?

Michael (*eagerly*) Whisky, please.

Joyce I'll have a gin and tonic.

George prepares the drinks

Everything's on now, so I'll just sit down for a minute before I get ready.

George You do that, Joyce. You deserve a break.

Joyce Only five minutes, though. I must get changed.

Michael You look fine to me.

Joyce My hair's a mess.

Michael It's never a mess, Joyce. You have the kind of hair that always looks soft and natural.

Joyce Why don't you ever say things like that, George?

George I do, but you don't believe me. It's the husband's lot to have his compliments smashed back at him like tennis balls.

Michael (*to Joyce*) You've lost weight as well, haven't you?

George He shoots, he scores!

Joyce (*glaring at George*) As a matter of fact, I *have*. A couple of pounds or more.

George I wish I understood why you put yourself through this endless agony about your weight, Joyce. In all the years we've known each other you've never looked any different. And yet there's this constant pinching of flesh in front of the mirror, the endless hours at the gym, and worst of all the hideous tension of the Friday morning weighing session. An ounce either way can dictate the tone of my whole weekend, Mike. You've no idea of the suspense.

Joyce You wouldn't love me if I was fat.

George I most certainly would.

Michael I merely pointed out that your wife looked a touch thinner, George.

Joyce Thank you, Michael. It's nice to know that my efforts to keep trim are appreciated by *someone*.

Michael Pert is the word I'd use to describe you, Joyce.

George I'd quit while you're ahead if I was you.

Joyce It's a very long time since you described me as pert.

George I don't think I ever have. Pert. It sounds like a small bird, doesn't it? The Lesser Spotted Pert.

Joyce Please don't go rambling off on one of your verbal excursions, George. They give me a headache.

Michael (*swallowing his whisky and looking anxiously at the champagne*) Do you think it's cold enough yet?

Joyce I'll have a feel.

George I think the colder the better. Frozen solid might be safest.

Joyce I think you're being extremely rude. It was very kind of Michael to bring it. I'm sure it was very expensive.

Michael Surprisingly reasonable actually. (*He pauses*) Shall we open it, then?

Joyce Well ... shouldn't we wait for Helen?

Michael Didn't I tell you? Helen's not coming.

Joyce Why not?

Michael Oh, she's umpiring some kind of wrestling match between sterling and the dollar.

Joyce Well, isn't she coming on later?

Michael (*vaguely*) She didn't say anything about it...

George You did ask her, didn't you?

Joyce Of course he did.

Michael (*unconvincingly*) Of course I did.

Joyce It's very inconsiderate. But that's Helen all over. (*She pauses*) Well, then, champagne it is. You can do the honours, Michael.

Michael stands up, unwrapping the foil

Michael The thing with champagne is to hold the cork still and revolve the bottle. (*He struggles with it but the cork shows no interest in budging*) Well, that's true for *French* champagne, of course. They may do things differently in Eastern Europe. (*He cocks the bottle on his hip and pushes the cork with his thumb*)
George (*alarmed*) Would you mind pointing that somewhere else?
Michael Sorry. (*He swings the bottle round*)

Joyce cowers nervously. Michael makes a huge but severely uncoordinated effort

Stand back, everybody!

He finally manages to dislodge the cork, which flops to the floor with a disappointing plop. Not so much as a drop emerges from the bottle

(*After a moment*) Superior bottling technique, I expect. (*He pours the wine, which is conspicuously flat*) Well, cheers!
Joyce To your film!
George Hear, hear.

They drink

Long pause

Michael Interesting.
Joyce Is it me or is there something rather unusual in the bouquet?
George There's a particular fish I'm trying to put my finger on...
Joyce (*briskly*) I think it's very nice.
George "Extraordinary" is the word I'd use.
Joyce (*glaring at George*) So, Michael, what happens when you've made your film?
Michael I expect we'll put it in the Cannes Film Festival.
Joyce Cannes. How wonderful. All those topless super-models.
Michael And after that, who knows? I expect I'll have to live in Los Angeles. That's really where the action is in the film business.
George You'll be a mover and shaker.
Michael (*smiling*) I'll try a little moving first to see how it feels. If I don't feel any ill effects I might do some cautious shaking after that.

Joyce Are you listening to this, George?

George I thought I was, darling, but I suspect from your tone I may not be picking up the subtext.

Joyce Los Angeles. Michael is going to live in *Los Angeles*.

George I don't think he said it quite that categorically…

Joyce And here we are marooned in Croydon. (*She pauses*) I expect you'll have a swimming pool, Michael?

Michael I hadn't really thought. Most people do out there.

Joyce (*venomously*) There you are, George, a *swimming pool*. (*She takes a long sip of her drink. The alcohol has a rapid effect on her*) I admire you, Michael. I really do.

Michael Thank you very much, Joyce. I admire you too.

Joyce You know how to go out and get what you want. You're an *achiever*. (*She pauses*) Frankly I find it incredible sometimes that you and my husband are related. I mean, George is one of those people who watches everything from the sidelines, whereas you—well, you're … what's the word for it?

George (*helpfully*) Dynamic?

Joyce Dynamic. Exactly. Why can't you be dynamic, George?

George (*reasonably*) It beats me.

Joyce Michael would never allow me to be abused by an *arriviste* thug in a Range Rover.

Michael Sorry?

Joyce I was always attracted to active people. I can't understand how I managed to end up married to a man with all the get-up and go of the average slug. (*She finishes her glass and pours herself another one*) This really isn't bad when you get used to it.

George And you probably don't need enamel on your teeth anyway.

Joyce narrows her eyes and focuses tipsily on George as though lining him up in a rifle-sight

Joyce You know, George, people are always telling me how *nice* you are.

George That's good of them.

Joyce Shall I tell you what I reply? I say that "nice" is another word for being taken advantage of. "Nice" is always at the back of the queue. "Nice" is twelve years on the same Civil Service grade. (*She pauses*) I'm sick and tired of "nice", George. I wouldn't care if you were a complete and utter bastard. I just wish you'd *do* something. (*She gets up, swaying dangerously, then looks at them with enormous dignity*) I am going for my shower.

Joyce walks unsteadily to the door and goes out

Michael (*awe-struck*) Wow.

George Alcohol doesn't really agree with her.

Michael I'm surprised it's that brave. (*He pauses*) She's … ferocious when she picks up speed, isn't she?

George Oh yes, a real typhoon. If you haven't tied yourself to something solid you're liable to be swept up and slapped down half a mile away.

Michael (*visibly impressed*) Still, I see what you mean about being beautiful when she's angry. She was actually *radiant*. (*He pauses, then muses*) I don't think I've ever noticed before.

George Noticed what?

Michael That Joyce is so … well, that's she's really very… (*More cautiously*) It doesn't matter. I'm just rambling. Give me another glass of that champagne-style drink, would you?

By now George is tipsy and Michael well on the way to being blind drunk

Was that just a routine going-over or are you in the doghouse for any particular reason?

George I think it's something to do with the fence.

Michael Of course. What else?

George Not so much the fence *specifically*. It just seems to have taken on a kind of symbolic value. Painting it, I mean.

Michael Don't you want to?

George I do … it's just that I'm not very good at that type of thing. Well, you know that.

Michael True. I can still remember the way you glued the arm back on my Action Man. It looked like he had a trunk.

George I'd like to be handier round the house. I know it would make Joyce's life easier, but it's a skill I've never acquired.

Michael You could change if you wanted to.

George Oh, no. I don't think so. Some things in life you just can't do.

Michael Rubbish. You can do anything if you set your mind to it. It's just a matter of will-power.

George There must be more to it than that.

Michael It's purely a question of self-image. If your *image* of yourself is of a clumsy idiot, that's what you'll be. All you have to do is change the image.

George That's all there is to it?

Michael Certainly. The key to success in any field is positive thinking.

George It's a nice idea. The problem is that positive thinking's difficult when your mind's a blank. Confronted by a hammer, a nail and a piece of wood I'm like a crashed computer.

Michael The only way you're going to give Joyce what she wants is by changing your mental attitude, George. You have to think to yourself "I *can* do it".

George I *can* do it.

Michael That's all it takes.

George You might be right. It's just that a lifetime's experience tells me the contrary.

Michael Expel the negative.

George All right. If you say so.

Michael Think how much better it'll make things with Joyce.

Joyce now appears in the doorway. She is in a gown and has a towel around her neck. Her hair hangs around her face, sopping wet. She holds her hairdryer up accusingly

Joyce (*deadly calm*) If one of you would find me a mallet, I'm just popping out to the garden for a moment.

George Oh, God.

Joyce A dog in this condition would be put down. I'm only applying the same logic.

Michael Playing up, is it?

Joyce (*with immense self-control*) Just a touch.

Michael looks significantly at George, who takes a second to grasp his meaning

George Oh, I don't know...

Michael This is your chance.

George You really think so?

Michael *Carpe diem.*

George (*suddenly determined*) There's no need to terminate that hairdryer, Joyce.

Joyce Why not?

George Because I'm going to fix it.

Joyce looks at him in astonishment. George goes across and takes it from her, holding it as though dealing with a lethal snake

Joyce You're going to fix it?

George That's what I said. (*He turns to look back at Michael*) I *can* do it.

Michael gives him an encouraging thumbs up

George goes out

Joyce (*amazed*) What on earth's got into him?

Michael He's changing his self-image.

Joyce goes to the fireplace, rubbing her hair with the towel. Tousled, barefoot and in her gown, she looks very attractive

(*After a moment*) Why don't you let me do that?
Joyce I can manage.
Michael No, really. Let me.

Joyce hesitates then gives him the towel, sitting stiffly on the floor in front of him

Why not have another drink?
Joyce I think I will. (*She pours the last of the bottle for them both*) What were you and George talking about?
Michael Nothing much.
Joyce (*from under the towel*) I used to love this. Sitting in front of the fire with Mother drying my hair.
Michael (*after a moment*) Are you all right now?
Joyce What do you mean?
Michael You seemed a little put-out a moment ago.
Joyce Other women have working hairdryers, Michael. Other women have husbands who paint the fence and fix the gutter and compete for the parking space at the front of the house. (*She pauses*) You must think I'm an awful bitch.
Michael Of course not.
Joyce You probably tell everyone you're closely related to a dragon.
Michael We all get frustrated sometimes, Joyce.
Joyce It's just the way George never fights back. He simply sits there like some great smiling Buddha, refusing to be provoked. I know I behave dreadfully to him every now and then. I can hear myself doing it. But I can't stop. (*She pauses*) Why is good nature so annoying sometimes?
Michael Because we're all human. We want people to be as bad as us; that way we feel reassured. Good people only remind us how imperfect we are.

Joyce comes out from under the towel to look at him

Joyce If I didn't know you better, I'd say that was perilously close to wisdom. (*She pauses*) Don't stop. It's nice.

He begins to rub her head again, more deliberately this time. She relaxes against his knees

The truth is, I shouldn't have married him. There, I've said it now. Someone else would have made him happier.

Michael Oh, I think George is all right. What you mean is, someone else would have made *you* happier.
Joyce I suppose I do.

There is a long awkward moment of silence. He puts the towel to one side

But my motto's always been, once you make a decision you should stick with it.

George's booming voice cuts in from upstairs

George (*off; shouting*) Do we have any pliers? Nail scissors don't seem to work. (*He pauses*) No, wait, hang on. Got it. OK.
Joyce (*to Michael*) Don't you think you should go and help him out?
Michael I'm happy where I am. (*He pauses*) I don't think *I've* ever stuck with a decision in my life.
Joyce I don't believe that. You always seem so certain of what you want.
Michael I am now.

She turns to look at him, slipping back accidentally against his inner thigh as she does so. She is now leaning against him quite heavily and he's making no effort to move

Joyce...
Joyce (*trying to stand up*) I have quite definitely had too much to drink...

Michael catches her arm and holds it

Michael It's not just the drink, Joyce. You feel it too, don't you?
Joyce Feel what?
Michael This thing.
Joyce Thing?
Michael Thing.
Joyce This is silly. I'm Joyce. Your older sister.
Michael Sister-in-law. And not much older. (*He pauses*) I don't know why but I've never really looked at you before, Joyce. You're really quite stunning.
George (*off; shouting*) Is it green and yellow into the live socket or brown? No, wait, cancel that, I had the book upside-down.

Pause

Any minute now, Joycie, your hair-drying problems will be solved forever.

Joyce (*to Michael*) Nobody in my whole life has told me I'm stunning before.
Michael Well, they should have.
Joyce You don't mean it.
Michael I do.
Joyce You're drunk.
Michael Completely smashed. (*He pauses*) But I still have this overwhelming
  urge to slip that gown over your shoulders and make love to you on the floor
  right now.
Joyce (*after a long pause*) The carpet hasn't been shampooed for ages.

They stare at each other, mesmerised

George (*off*) There's nothing to this, you know, Mike! Amazing how it all
  fits together. Just one more slight adjustment...
Joyce I've always ... noticed you, Michael. But in an affectionate way... I
  mean, you're handsome, of course ... extremely handsome... I admit in
  idle moments I've sometimes speculated on what those wonderful tummy
  muscles of yours might feel like ... purely as a sister does ... but never in
  my wildest dreams did I think you might harbour...

*He kisses her lingeringly on the mouth. She stares at him, confused by a lust
as overwhelming as it is unexpected*

Do you really think the floor is a good idea?

He kisses her again

George will be down in a moment... (*Her voice trails off*)

He holds his arms out to her

I simply had no idea you felt this way.

*They fall on each other passionately. Joyce, transformed by desire, is just
pushing him back on the sofa*

George (*off*) You were right, Mike! Nothing to it at all when you put your
  mind to it. Here we go. Five, four, three, two, one—lift off!

*There is an enormous bang and a flash as the Lights go out at once. The stage
is completely silent, except for an electric buzz in the darkness*

SCENE 3

George, again in his dark suit and racy tie, is spotlit, with the rest of the stage in darkness

George I admit it didn't end too well in this case, but I still think Mike was right. It's never too late to change. Of course, in my case you'd probably say it fairly obviously is, and you wouldn't be alone. That's certainly the attitude I've been encountering on this side since it all happened. That's why when I explained what I wanted to do they all looked a bit sceptical. There's a general feeling the practical approach isn't really my thing. But, as I said to them, just because you're dead it doesn't mean you can't improve yourself. They didn't look convinced, but at least they were willing to let me have a go.

The Lights go up on the living-room. We are back where we left Scene 1

A terrified Michael is on the floor, curled in a tight foetal ball, peeking up through his fingers at George

Michael Go away!
George You look pretty daft down there, you know.
Michael You're not here.
George Oh, I think I am.

Michael stares at his brother incredulously. George is mildly embarrassed by the scrutiny

Michael You're dead.
George Technically I suppose that's true.
Michael Technically?
George Well, not just technically. (*He beams good-humouredly at Michael*)

Michael looks at him carefully, then edges along the sofa to the jelly bowls. He picks up the two dessert spoons, then rushes at George with a blood-curdling yell, the spoons in the form of a crucifix. He stops about an inch away

I'm dead, Mike, not a vampire. (*He pauses*) I really have upset you, haven't I? I knew I shouldn't have done that little trick with the lights. I just wanted you to see I've got the hang of this electricity thing.
Michael I'm definitely drinking too much.
George Well, the drink helps, of course.
Michael Helps what?

George It makes it easier for me to get through to you.

Michael OK, that's it. I'm now going to concentrate hard on waking myself up. (*He squeezes his eyes closed, then opens them again slowly*)

George smiles patiently

Oh God, I knew I shouldn't have watched *It's A Wonderful Life* again when I got back from the pub the other night. My subconscious is getting everything mixed up.

George (*nostalgically*) "Every time a bell rings another angel gets its wings."

Michael I know, I know. And now you're going to show me how much worse off everyone would be if I'd never lived.

George I'm not sure you'd come out of that exercise quite as well as James Stewart, Mike.

Michael I don't understand any of this.

George I was just trying to explain...

Michael Well, don't. I'm having a terrible day. I'm in shock, I'm drunk and now I'm hallucinating.

George I really have shaken you up, haven't I?

Michael (*querulously*) You've frightened the life out of me. You're still doing it.

George smiles apologetically and goes over to the sofa

George It's very nice to see you, Mike. It really is.

Michael What are you doing here, anyway?

George Oh, just floating about.

Michael Well, can't you go and haunt someone else?

George I don't think so. I'm pretty sure no-one else is allowed to see me.

Michael Why me? Why not Joyce?

George Oh, Joyce isn't the type to believe in ghosts.

Michael Neither am I!

George Oh, come on, Mike. Anyone who thinks that Sylvester Stallone would make a good English aristocrat will believe anything.

Michael He has got range, you know.

Pause

(*Looking at him closely*) That's a repulsive tie you're wearing, by the way.

George It's the one I was buried in. Birthday present. Joyce could never get me to wear it when I was alive.

Michael She likes to have the last word, doesn't she?

George That's Joyce. (*He pauses*) She was pretty magnificent at the funeral, wasn't she?

Michael You've been around the whole time, have you?

George Pretty much.

Michael You might be able to help then. Is it me or is there something odd about the way Joyce is behaving?

George How do you mean?

Michael She keeps looking at me in a very significant way. As though she's *expecting* something from me. And I can't for the life of me think what it might be.

George You are drinking too much, Mike.

Michael Why? What have I forgotten?

George The night I short-circuited half of Surrey? Ring any bells?

Michael Well, it was terrible, what with you electrocuting yourself and then afterwards having to deal with the hospital and the police, and phoning everyone...

George You don't remember what happened just before it all started?

Michael There was a lot of drinking ... you were rabbiting on about the fence for some reason...

George That's all?

Michael You had a row, I remember that ... then Joyce went up to have a shower—that's why she was wearing her gown under her coat at the hospital—she went up to have a shower, and then she came down ... and then... (*He stops*) And then ... oh no, no, no, no, no. Oh God. I did something, didn't I?

George You unleashed forces way beyond your control.

Michael I made a pass at her.

George Exactly.

Michael (*wailing*) But it was nothing personal. I do that to everyone.

George Try telling Joyce that.

Michael What was I thinking? (*He pauses*) She didn't take it seriously, did she?

George I don't think you need me to help you with that one.

Michael Yes, of course she did. Dear God, what am I going to say to her? (*He suddenly stops, staring at George in surprise*) Wait a minute. How do you know all this, anyway? You were upstairs the whole time.

George It seems to come with the territory. You just ... know things.

Michael looks at George in poorly concealed alarm

Michael It's not why you're here, is it?

George What?

Michael You're not thinking of doing anything rash?

George Oh, you think I've come all the way back here just to sink my talons in, rip your entrails out and drag you off screaming to Hell?

Michael (*after a moment*) That's putting it more colourfully than I had in mind.

George Oh, God, no, *of course* not. What an absurd idea.

Michael You're not jealous, then?

George Well, I might be if I was alive. But in my present condition that type of thing doesn't seem to matter any more.

Michael You're above it all, you mean?

George Not so much that. You just have a general sense of well-being towards everyone.

Michael Even me?

George Oh, especially you, Mike. I love you. You're my brother.

Michael (*moved*) Thank you. (*He pauses*) I'm really sorry about what happened, by the way. Did it hurt?

George Can't remember much about it. But I'll tell you one thing. (*He leans forward conspiratorially, his tone dramatic*) You know when people talk about floating above your body, and then seeing a bright white light in the distance and wanting to move towards it?

Michael (*eagerly*) Yes?

George Utter balls.

Michael That's a pity. It always sounded rather nice. (*He pauses. He is getting used to George's presence*) What's it like, then? Being dead?

George Oh, much the same as being alive, only you get in free at the cinema.

Michael (*smiling, then awkwardly*) I feel terrible about the whole bloody disaster. I should have known you couldn't do it.

George (*smiling; without rancour*) Still, you had to find a way to get me out of the room if you were going to seduce Joyce successfully.

Michael looks down with genuine contrition

Michael This is all my fault. If it wasn't for me you wouldn't be dead.

George (*kindly*) Don't be too hard on yourself, Mike. It's not as though you were *trying* to kill me.

Michael wants to say more but can't

Michael So ... what happens now?

George Hmmmm?

Michael I assume you're not going to stay here forever?

George Oh, no. Just a day or two, as far as I know.

Michael As far as you know?

George They don't tell you much. It's frighteningly bureaucratic. A bit like being back at the office frankly, only without that clever new computer system.

Michael They? Who's they?
George That's classified, I'm afraid.

Michael shakes his head in disbelief

Michael I'm not really having this conversation. It's ludicrous. I'm asleep.
    This is a dream and any minute now I'm going to wake up. (*He closes his
    eyes and lies down on the sofa. After a moment he looks up*)

George smiles at him calmly. Michael bounces up gamely

    Right then, if you really are here you can answer a few questions.
George I'll do my best.
Michael What about Heaven? Is there one?
George (*gently*) Of course there is.
Michael What's it like?
George That's tricky. It's such a personal thing. But put it this way. It's not
    the kind of place where England lose to Argentina in penalty shoot-outs.
Michael Ha! So God *is* an Englishman.
George Well, in *my* version of Heaven, yes.
Michael So what you mean is, Heaven changes for people depending on who
    they are and what they want?
George Well, one person's idea of Heaven isn't the same as another's, is it?
    It would be pretty difficult to come up with a single concept to please
    everybody.
Michael (*uneasily*) What about Hell?
George Don't you think we get enough Hell on earth, Mike?
Michael Is that a definitive "no"?
George You look concerned.
Michael Of course I'm not. I think I'm a pretty decent guy on the whole. I've
    got every reason to be confident on the Paradise front. It's just that you
    never know how strict the entry qualifications are going to be.
George I don't think you deserve to go to Hell, Mike. (*He pauses*) Do you?

Michael looks unnerved by this

Michael Well, look, don't you feel *any* different?
George Apart from being dead? Not really.
Michael But you *do* have all the answers now?
George Oh, yes. Absolutely. Big Bang, Meaning of Life, the whole shooting
    match.
Michael Well, go on then.
George Mmm. Bit difficult to explain. But that Stephen Hawking book is
    very good.

Michael Look, George, it's not that I'm not pleased to see you, but why *are* you here?

George Just trying to make sure it's a smooth transition for everybody.

Michael You mean you're going to put a winning lottery ticket in Joyce's pocket or something?

George only laughs at this idea. Michael looks at him in mounting frustration

You must have some kind of plan?

George (*evasively*) Oh, I wouldn't call it a plan, exactly.

Michael decides to come at the issue from another angle

Michael But this is all about me?

George What makes you say that?

Michael Because if it wasn't I imagine you'd be haunting someone else!

George I'm *appearing* to you, Mike. That doesn't mean this is *about* you.

Michael Oh. That's good.

George Of course, it doesn't mean it isn't, either.

Michael Well, that makes me feel *much* better.

George I really think you're worrying far too much about all this. If I were you I'd just carry on with whatever you were going to do. Don't give me a second thought. (*He sits back placidly*)

Michael stares at him balefully

Oh, don't worry, I won't even be around most of the time. And I can't influence your behaviour directly anyway. We're not allowed to interfere, you see. I should have mentioned that before. Even that business with the lights was pushing it a bit. (*He pauses*) No, look, I really don't want to mess up your evening. I mean, what about your assignation with Debbie?

Michael (*startled*) You know about that as well, do you?

George I have to admit I admire your tenacity, Mike, I mean, going for the full set of sisters. What a trouper.

Michael Joyce doesn't really count.

George That's not very chivalrous.

Michael I don't mean she isn't attractive. But she is your wife.

George That didn't cut much ice last time.

Michael The truth is if I hadn't been drunk I'd never have made a pass at her.

George Is that what you're going to tell her?

Michael Probably. If the subject comes up.

George I have a feeling it might. (*He pauses. Quietly*) She set a lot of store by what you said to her, you know.

Michael I don't suppose you can remember what it was, by any chance?
George I expect you can guess. Your repertoire isn't very extensive, is it?
Michael Isn't it?
George A couple of perfunctory compliments followed by a determined lunge. Not the kind of thing that's going to give Cyrano de Bergerac many sleepless nights. It must be the fact that you do it with such conviction that appeals to them all.
Michael Plus the good looks. They must count for something.
George Up to a point, I admit. But your real trick is that you have a gift for making women believe you even when you're being totally insincere.
Michael I wouldn't say I was ever *insincere*, exactly.
George Oh, come on. You'd say absolutely anything to get a woman into bed.
Michael (*triumphantly*) Yes, but I always mean it at the time.

George looks at him sardonically. Michael can't hold his gaze

George If you light the fuse, Mike, it's no good looking surprised when the bomb goes off.
Michael (*self-pityingly*) I am in the market for the right person, you know. I'd like to be with someone who really understands me. (*He pauses*) If I found the right woman, I don't think I'd have any problem being faithful. (*He pauses*) I suppose I am a bit of a shit, aren't I?
George (*genuinely dismayed*) Oh, God, no! I think you're a terrific bloke. (*He pauses*) Listen, I really shouldn't keep you talking. Debbie's going to fall asleep if you don't get up there soon.
Michael You really think I should go up to see her?
George You're in love with her, aren't you?

Michael looks at him uneasily

Well, that's what you *said*. And it's obvious she's crazy about you.
Michael (*getting up*) There's nothing to stop me going?
George Nothing at all.
Michael (*hesitating*) Still, I don't know ... she is a wonderful girl ... it's just...
George What?
Michael I'm not sure it's the right thing to do.
George Why on earth not?
Michael Because I'm *not* in love with her. I was only saying that to get her into bed. (*He pauses*) I *fancy* her, all right, but I think she really loves me and if I go ahead and sleep with her I'm pretty sure I'll break her heart.
George I see. (*He pauses*) She's up there waiting, Mike. She's awfully keen. Are you sure you want to disappoint her?

Michael (*with difficulty*) I think I'll stay down here.

George Fair enough. That's your final decision, is it?

Michael (*with growing determination*) Yes.

George Not that it's really any of my business, but I'm sure you're doing the right thing.

Michael Thanks. (*He pauses*) We can just stay here and chat.

George I'd love to, Mike, but I'm afraid I can't stop. Things to do.

Michael I was just beginning to enjoy myself.

George (*getting up*) Me too. (*He pauses*) Well, I better be off, then. See you, Mike.

Michael George——

The Lights go down

George exits

The Lights go up again to reveal Michael on his own in the room. He starts, as though woken from a dream

George? (*He looks around, then crosses to the light switch, which works normally. He searches the room, satisfying himself there is no-one there. He shakes his head like a dog, then picks up his glass of whisky from the coffee table*) It'll be fluorescent spiders next. (*He knocks back the whisky in one gulp, then laughs*) I should have known it was a dream, George. That thing about us beating Argentina was a dead give-away. (*He pauses*) Oh my God, Debbie! (*He makes a move, then stops, deeply uneasy. He tries to convince himself*) What's wrong with two grown-up people having a little fun together, for God's sake? (*He hesitates, torn between staying and going, perching uncertainly on the edge of the sofa*) We both know where we stand. She's perfectly well aware I'm still involved with Helen. (*He pauses. Angrily*) It was a dream. (*He gets up with a new air of determination*) Stay right where you are, Debbie, I'm on the way. (*His bravado lasts only as far as the door. He pauses without opening it, in an agony of indecision. He looks around*) George? (*He waits with his hand on the doorknob*)

There is no reply. The Lights go down

CURTAIN

ACT II

Scene 1

Lights come up on Michael creeping along the hall. The music is tense and nerve-tingling, creating a rising sense of tension

He knocks softly on Debbie's door

Debbie opens it immediately and flings herself into his arms

Debbie Oh, Michael, I knew you'd come. I love you so much.
Michael Of course you do.
Debbie You can do anything you want with me.
Michael Anything?

She nods wholeheartedly

   Joyce and Helen appear

Joyce Michael!

Michael and Debbie spring apart guiltily

Helen Debbie! How could you!
Joyce (*to Michael*) You betrayed me.
Helen You? What about me?
Debbie Michael loves me.
Joyce Rubbish. He loves me.
Helen Do I have a say in this?
Joyce You've betrayed us all, Michael. (*She pauses*) You've got to be stopped. You're a danger to women everywhere. (*She produces a kitchen knife from her gown and advances on him menacingly*)
Michael Joyce! No…

As the music reaches a frantic climax, she raises the knife above her head and plunges it repeatedly into Michael's chest

   Oh my God! (*He sinks to the floor*)

Debbie rushes to him, then looks up in horror

Debbie He's dead! Michael's dead!

Helen glances indifferently at the corpse, then coolly lights a cigarette

Hold on the tableau for a moment before the Lights go down abruptly. With the rest of the stage in darkness, the Lights go up on George, in funeral clothes and striking tie. He shakes his head sadly

George Poor Mike. I suppose there was always a risk of something like that happening one day. I tried to warn him. Joyce isn't the type to take that kind of humiliation lying down. (*He looks sadly at the audience for a further moment, then smiles broadly*) Oh, all right. It didn't really happen, or rather, it did, but only in Mike's sub-conscious. Actually, he's still in the living-room now, mulling things over, trying to choose between lust and fear—and if I know my brother there's only going to be one winner. So it could all still happen, maybe not quite like that but perhaps just as disastrously in some other way. That's why I spoke to the people here about going back for a while. I told them all it needed was a little helping hand to point things in the right direction. They weren't confident, but they could see I had the family's best interests at heart—and I think they reckoned I deserved one last chance to show I could do the practical thing when it really matters. After all, no-one wants to go into infinity with "clumsy oaf" stamped on their file. (*He pauses. Less confidently*) Now all I have to do is make sure I don't make a hash of it.

SCENE 2

Michael creeps silently along the hall

Helen enters

He stands frozen in horror

Helen Michael! You made me jump. What are you doing?
Michael Hmmm?
Helen I said, what are you doing?
Michael Oh ... going to the loo.
Helen You don't seem to be making much progress.
Michael I heard you coming in. I didn't want to move in case I gave you a shock.

Helen You *did* give me a shock, lurking about in the darkness like that.

Michael If I'd kept going it might have been worse.

Helen You thought if you stood absolutely still I might just pass by without noticing you?

Michael I hadn't really thought it through. It was instinctive.

Helen Look, I know it's been a difficult day, but don't drink any more, will you? I'm worried about the amount you put away. I don't want you turning into one of those people who wanders about Soho dribbling and screaming abuse.

Michael In Soho that's the best way of blending in. (*He pauses, then tries to move to safer territory*) So, how are the money markets?

Helen Unstable. But at least the dollar's holding steady.

Michael God bless America.

Helen With my luck it would have chosen today to plunge.

Michael You've never really got over Black Wednesday, have you?

Helen You can joke, but the whole experience was shattering. Interest rates go ballistic and what am I doing? Sitting in a health hydro in Reykjavik covered in mud.

Michael Everyone has to relax sometimes, Hel. Even you.

Helen You know what they say on the trading floor. Relaxation is just another word for missed opportunities.

They smile wryly at each other

Michael Still, your skin did look lovely when you came back.

Helen You took one look and launched yourself at me. We didn't get out of bed for the entire weekend.

Michael I'd missed you——

Helen It's a long time since we did something like that.

Michael You're always so busy.

Helen (*sharply*) You're always so drunk.

Michael I wasn't criticizing you, Hel.

Helen No. I'm sorry. It's just tiredness. (*She pauses*) We didn't always fight, did we, Mike? Not in the beginning, at any rate. There was a time when we suited each other pretty well. You used to like the fact that I had a career that mattered to me.

Michael That was before it took you over.

Helen I haven't changed.

Michael I don't think I'm any different either, really, it's just that what *you* used to say was charming and spontaneous now irritates the hell out of you.

They look at each other helplessly

Helen Look, Michael, I don't know what was going on between you and

Debbie, and I don't think I want to any more. Just tell me now, quite straightforwardly, do you want to carry on seeing me or not?

Michael stares at her, paralysed by indecision

If it's over, let's just face it and move on. No blame, no recrimination. (*She pauses*) I'll make it easy for you. Do you still love me? Yes or no?

Michael (*after a long moment*) Well, of *course* I do.

Helen Oh. (*She pauses. Her manner softens*) Look, I'm sorry there's only a single bed in my room.

Michael It's all right.

Helen You know what I'm like about my comfort, but ... if you wanted to come in for a moment on the strict understanding that you leave straight afterwards, I suppose that would be all right.

Michael Ummm ... perhaps not tonight.

Helen (*ruefully*) That wasn't the most romantic of invitations, was it?

Michael smiles. Helen has the grace to laugh at herself. She kisses him lightly

Goodnight.

Michael Night. (*He walks back towards the living-room*)

Helen I thought you wanted the loo?

Michael The moment's passed.

Helen goes off

Michael waits, then runs back along the hall to Debbie's door

(*Whispering*) Debbie?

The Lights go up in the bedroom, where Debbie sits on a rickety-looking camp bed reading a magazine. She wears a large pair of men's pyjamas. She looks up and rushes to open the door

Debbie I'd just about given you up.

Michael I fell asleep.

Debbie That's flattering.

Michael Still, I'm here now. (*He pauses*) I like your jim-jams.

Debbie I didn't bring the lacy black négligé. I didn't think I'd need it.

Michael No, those are great. I've always found women in pyjamas overwhelmingly sexy. I think it's the result of seeing too many Doris Day films at an impressionable age.

Debbie I'll take them off, shall I?

Michael We're going straight at it, then?

Debbie Well ... not if you don't want to... I just thought you might want to ... you know ... get moving. Sorry. I'm a bit nervous.

Michael That's all right.

Debbie I've fantasised about this happening for so long that now it is I can't quite believe it. I didn't mean to rush anything.

Michael No, it's fine. You're right. After all, it *is* why I'm here, isn't it? (*He opens his arms to her*)

Debbie holds him tightly

Debbie Are you sure you're still keen?

Michael (*distracted*) Of course I am. Can I tell you something? (*He pauses*) A moment ago I dreamed I was talking to George.

Debbie I suppose it's only natural.

Michael It was astonishingly vivid. He hadn't changed a bit. And he was wearing the most extraordinary tie. (*He pauses*) Sorry, where were we?

Debbie Warming up.

Michael Oh, yes. (*He kisses her*)

She breaks away shyly

Debbie Perhaps we should get into bed? (*She gets into the camp bed*)

Michael takes off his shirt and trousers and goes to join her. The bed is very narrow. Debbie wriggles to one side to make a space for him. Michael sits tentatively on the edge, which makes the bed tip upwards on the other side

We need a counter-weight. I'm not heavy enough.

Michael I think the key is an even distribution of weight. If I jump on and land squarely there shouldn't be a problem.

Debbie Isn't there a risk I might get squashed?

Michael I'll land with all four limbs extended, like a cat. That way you'll be safe underneath.

Debbie (*amused*) Maybe you should get in first. You're heavier than me so the bed won't tip up when I follow you.

Michael Brilliant.

Debbie gets out while Michael gets in cautiously. Debbie sits on the edge of the frame, then rolls awkwardly on top of him. Their combined weight is too much for the bed which immediately collapses inwards under the strain, leaving only the frame intact. They emerge from the bedclothes

Debbie Do you think it's got any further to go?

Michael I think that's it. Are you all right?
Debbie Fine.

Michael puts his arms around her and they kiss

George enters and stands in the far corner of the room, smiling

Michael is just about to roll over on top of Debbie when he sees George

Michael Aaaaaaggghhhhh!

Debbie is unable to see or hear George

Debbie Michael? What is it?
Michael (*to George*) What the hell are you doing here?
Debbie What do you mean?
George Just thought I'd pop by to see how you were doing.
Michael Go away!
Debbie It's my bedroom!
Michael (*concentrating desperately*) I wasn't talking to you.
Debbie What do you mean? Who were you talking to?
Michael I was having a ... hallucination.
Debbie What of?
Michael (*frantically*) A dog...
Debbie What?
Michael I was attacked by a dog when I was little. I... I sometimes get flashbacks at times of stress.
Debbie I thought you said it was a hallucination.
Michael It *feels* like a hallucination ... really it's more of a terrible memory. That's it. I've got Recovered Memory Syndrome.
Debbie (*sceptically*) Recovered Memory Syndrome?
Michael It's awful. One moment you're strolling along perfectly happily, the next you're lying flattened under a pile of hideous memories.
Debbie What kind of dog was it?
Michael What kind? (*He panics*) It was a ... dachshund.
Debbie A sausage dog! That doesn't sound very frightening.
Michael I *was* very small at the time ... all I can remember is snarling teeth ... terrible pain in the ankle ... blood everywhere... (*He pauses*) The details are a blur. (*He pauses. To George*) I was just telling it to *go away*.
George Don't worry, Mike, she can't see me.
Debbie (*to Michael*) Are you having treatment for it?
Michael No. (*He pauses*) Yes.
Debbie You don't sound very sure.

Michael I am sure, I'd just forgotten. That's the problem with the syndrome. One minute your memory's pin-sharp, the next... (*He pauses*) Of course, I remember now, I have to take drugs to control the memories. I must have forgotten my pill today. I better go and get it.

Debbie Michael, are you sure you're telling me the truth?

Michael Why wouldn't I?

Debbie I thought you might be looking for an excuse to get away.

Michael If I felt like that I wouldn't have come in the first place, would I?

Debbie I suppose not. (*She pauses*) I had no idea you were so tormented.

Michael (*with feeling*) Neither did I until recently. (*He goes to the door, making a frantic, repeated gesture to George to follow him*)

Only after a moment does he notice Debbie staring at him in puzzlement

(*To Debbie*) Nervous twitch. It's a side-effect of the medication.

George gives a thumbs-up of understanding to Michael, who opens the door. George follows him

The Lights go down on the extension and up in the hall

George I'm terribly sorry, Mike. That was tactless of me.

Michael You're not a dream.

George It's just that when you weren't in the living-room I thought I'd better look for you. I was worried.

Michael reaches out and pinches George's arm, which is only too solid

Michael Why is this happening to me?

George Haven't we been through that? (*He pauses*) So, you couldn't resist it, eh? I can't say I blame you. She's great, isn't she? So sweet and sincere.

Michael For God's sake keep your voice down.

George No-one else can hear me. You should know that by now. (*He shouts*) Hello! (*He pauses, then laughs*) A *dachshund*?

Michael (*with dignity*) I panicked.

George If you don't mind me asking, Mike, what changed your mind? I mean, you seemed so certain about not seeing her before.

Michael If there was a before—which I suppose I'm obliged to admit—I wasn't thinking straight. I was unnerved. Most people would be by the sudden appearance of a poltergeist.

George (*pedantically*) I'm a ghost, not a poltergeist. Poltergeists have this passion for rearranging the furniture—pretty pointless if you ask me, but dead people do have the most extraordinary range of interests.

Pause. Michael is looking at him balefully

Oh, I'm sorry. Do carry on.

Michael Debbie is a wonderfully attractive girl, whom I happen to want to sleep with. There is no reason on earth why I shouldn't. I refuse to be burdened with bourgeois sexual guilt.

George Fighting talk.

Michael (*less confidently*) So that's all right then, is it?

George Of course, if it's what you want.

Michael You're not going to try and stop me?

George I told you, I'm not allowed to interfere.

Michael Good. In that case, I'm going back in. OK?

George Fine.

Michael You realize it's going to be very difficult concentrating on the job in hand if there's any chance of you making a reappearance?

George Now I know where you are, I can rest easy.

Michael All right. Fine.

He holds up his hands in a "that's final" gesture in the same second that Helen appears in the hall

Michael stands petrified

Helen! Would you believe it? I did need the loo after all. (*He pauses*) Do you ever get that? When you're not sure if you want to go or not?

Helen (*stonily*) Who were you talking to just then?

Michael I was ... trying to find out if anyone was in the bathroom. You know how embarrassing it can be. Nobody ever locks the door behind them at night.

Helen Why didn't you just knock?

Michael I thought a loud knock might be frightening. If I whispered, whoever was inside would know it was me.

Helen stares at him for a long moment

Helen Michael, I want you to call Alcoholics Anonymous first thing in the morning. Now, for God's sake, go to bed.

Helen exits

Michael (*whispering to George*) I'm going back into Debbie's room now. *Alone*, if you don't mind.

George Point taken.

Michael gives him a last irritable glance, then raises his voice theatrically

Michael Goodnight, Helen!

He makes a shooing motion to George

  George goes off

Michael shoots back through Debbie's door like a bullet. The Lights cross-fade to her room

Debbie Are you all right?
Michael Fine. I just needed a moment for the medication to kick in.
Debbie You're so pale. I'm sorry if I didn't sound very sympathetic. It must be terrible having a condition like this.
Michael More terrible than you'll ever know.
Debbie (*softly*) Come back to bed. (*She pulls back the bedclothes invitingly*)

Michael looks around cautiously then sits next to her

  You look so young and vulnerable. It makes me want to wrap you up and protect you from the world.
Michael That would be nice.

Debbie begins to unbutton her pyjama top. Michael stops her

  I just need a minute to get my breath back.
Debbie I'm doing everything wrong, aren't I? I'm coy when I should be bold and brash when I should be sensitive. I knew I'd be no good with you.
Michael Don't say that. It's nothing to do with you.
Debbie Yes, it is. (*She pauses*) I used to be like this with Christmas. I'd look forward to it so much for weeks that when the day itself finally arrived I always felt exhausted and miserable.
Michael (*moved*) Do you really want me that much?
Debbie (*simply*) Always have done.
Michael (*guilty and anxious*) Look, it's not you. It's all my fault.
Debbie It's not your fault you have terrible memories.
Michael They're under control now.

Debbie rests her head on his chest

Debbie Do you think George would mind about us doing this tonight?
Michael He said he didn't.

Debbie What?

Michael I mean, I'm sure he wouldn't. You know how easygoing he was.

Debbie Some people might think it's a terrible way to behave.

Michael Helen, for one.

Debbie I know. And I do feel guilty about that. But you are going to tell her first thing in the morning that we love each other, aren't you?

Michael (*strangled*) Of course.

Debbie As long as we do love each other, nothing else really matters, does it?

Michael (*horribly uncomfortable*) No.

Debbie Have you got your breath back yet?

Michael It's well on the way.

Debbie Good. (*She kisses him*)

He is hesitant at first but then begins to respond. He shuts his eyes tightly

George enters and stands at the bottom of the bed

Michael opens his eyes

Michael (*shouting*) I thought I asked you not to do that!

Debbie I haven't done anything yet!

Michael Not you...

Debbie What do you mean, not me?

George I'm *terribly* sorry, Mike. I know this is hugely embarrassing. But I thought you might like to know that Joyce is on her way down to see you.

Michael What?

George She's just getting her robe on. If she finds you're not in the living-room there'll be a search party.

Michael (*leaping out of bed; frantically to George*) I'm with Helen!

Debbie I *know* you're with Helen, Michael, you don't have to rub it in.

Michael (*to Debbie*) I don't mean now... I mean... I mean...

Debbie What the hell do you mean?

George Joyce *knows* you're not with Helen, she just heard you saying goodnight.

Debbie (*angrily*) Michael, I don't understand what you're trying to say. Please, just tell me what's going on!

Michael (*desperately*) It's the dog again. I can hear it growling, in the corner. (*He pauses*) Telling it I'm with Helen usually makes it go away. It's frightened of her.

Debbie (*totally unconvinced*) It's obvious you've changed your mind about sleeping with me.

Michael I promise you, I'm telling the truth. It's not you, it's the dog.

Debbie All right then, why's it come back? You've taken your pill.

Michael (*with simulated shock*) They warned me this might happen. I'm developing an immunity.

Debbie is close to tears of frustration and wounded pride. Even in his abject panic, Michael has the grace to look guilty. He touches her face briefly

I'm sorry. Debbie. I've just got to take a booster and I'll be fine. (*He runs to the door*)
Debbie Don't come back unless you know what you really want.

The Lights go down on the extension and up on the hall. Michael hurtles out of Debbie's door, followed by George

Michael I thought you said you weren't allowed to interfere?
George Oh, it's defined pretty generously. I think they'd draw the line at dropping a vase on someone's head, but the odd word to the wise should be all right.

Joyce enters

Michael stands sweating and wide-eyed with panic

Michael Joyce!
George (*softly*) Hello, Joycie.

George watches Joyce affectionately as she moves towards Michael

Joyce I thought you'd be in bed, Michael.
Michael I was just on the way up to see Helen.
Joyce You've only just said goodnight to her.
Michael Have I? Are you sure?
Joyce I heard you.
Michael Perhaps I should check. You know what Helen's like over the small things. If I don't say goodnight properly she'll sulk for days.
Joyce Helen's perfectly all right, Michael.
Michael Is she? Well, that's a relief. The whole situation's been preying on my mind. I'll get to bed then.
Joyce Michael, we have to talk.
George Hello. Here it comes.
Michael Do we?
Joyce We do. No matter what's happened since, we can't take back what was said and done that night.
Michael I was afraid of that.

Joyce I'm grateful for your sensitivity. But on reflection I think now is as good a time as any. George would understand.

George Well, up to a point.

Joyce What I'm trying to say, Michael, is that I want you to feel free to speak your mind.

Michael (*wriggling on the hook*) Joyce, what happened that night was … astonishing…

Joyce It came as a surprise to me too, Michael. You'd never given the slightest indication you felt that way.

Michael I'd never been that drunk before.

Joyce What?

Michael I mean, the drink helped me lose my inhibitions. Of course, I'd always wanted to say it, but…

Joyce You had too much respect for my status as a married woman?

Michael Exactly.

Joyce We all need a little Dutch courage sometimes. I have to admit I wouldn't have got through today without a little something every now and then.

George I thought you were having trouble focusing, Joyce. I wondered if you'd forgotten to put your contacts in.

Michael (*forgetting*) I didn't know she wore contacts.

Joyce (*startled*) Who does?

Michael You do. (*He pauses*) Don't you?

Joyce Well … yes. I thought you were talking about someone else. You said "She".

Michael I … sometimes lapse into the third person at times of stress.

Joyce That's an odd habit.

Michael Isn't it? The Queen has a similar problem with the first person plural.

Joyce I suppose we're all suffering from stress today.

Michael Some of us more than others. (*He pauses. Quickly*) You, for example, Joyce. You really should be asleep.

Joyce I need to be with someone, Michael. I need to be with you. You can understand that, can't you?

Michael Of course I can.

Joyce You don't think I'm heartless?

Michael Never.

Joyce I suppose this would look appalling to an outsider. Me throwing myself at you on the night of my husband's funeral.

Michael Is that what you're doing?

Joyce Well … yes. Didn't you realize?

Michael Just checking.

Joyce All those things you said that night, the way you touched me… I can't

get it out of my head. I may be a little drunk but I know how I feel. I want
you, Michael.

George Look, I really think I should make myself scarce.

Michael (*panicking*) Don't go!

Joyce I'm not going anywhere if you don't want me to.

Michael Not you.

Joyce Not me what?

Michael I mean it's ... not you I should be with on a night like this. I have
to think of Helen.

Joyce Oh ... yes. Of course.

Michael She's very upset. I ought to be on hand to comfort her.

Joyce Oh God. I'm being very selfish, aren't I?

Michael No, you're not. None of us are thinking straight tonight.

George Speak for yourself.

Joyce Are you hot, Michael?

Michael Well, one or two people have said so...

Joyce You're sweating.

Michael wipes his hand across his forehead

Michael Oh ... so I am. (*He seizes on the opportunity*) Hyper-active sweat
glands, Joyce. It's an old problem. From June to September I'm as slippery
as an eel. And smelly too.

Joyce moves closer and sniffs his chest

Joyce You smell very nice.

Michael It can turn very quickly. One minute mountain dew, the next over-
ripe Camembert.

Joyce I think I'd be willing to take the chance.

Michael (*dejectedly*) Would you?

Joyce Yes. (*She pauses*) But there's always Helen to think about. What are
you going to do about Helen?

Michael At this precise moment in time, Joyce, I can honestly say I haven't
the faintest idea.

Joyce Perhaps you should just go up and have it out with her now.

Michael I don't think that would be wise.

Joyce No. I can see that. It's not the time. (*She pauses*) My God, what am
I saying? Of course it's not the time. Not for her, not for me, not for any
of us. (*She pauses*) Thank you, Michael. Thank you for reminding me how
to behave.

Michael Think nothing of it.

Joyce How much time do you think we should give it?

Michael Give it?

Joyce Before we tell the rest of the family of our intentions.

Michael I ... don't think we should rush into anything.

Joyce No. No. Of course not. (*She pauses*) Perhaps I should go to bed.

Michael Oh, would you, Joyce? Please?

Joyce Pardon?

Michael It's just that I think you'd feel so much better after a night's sleep. I'm worried about you.

Joyce (*kissing him*) That's very thoughtful.

Michael I do my best.

Joyce The funny thing is I don't really want to go back to my own bed. It has a George-sized hole in it. I keep putting out my hand and expecting him to be there. Silly, isn't it?

Michael (*gently*) I don't think it's silly, Joyce. Not at all.

Joyce I thought if I came down to you I wouldn't keep dwelling on it. But you're right. This isn't the time. (*She pauses, then gives him a steely look*) You did mean all those things you said the night George died, didn't you, Michael? You weren't just toying with me?

Michael I... I... (*He looks at George*) I meant everything I said, Joyce.

Joyce Including the part about slipping my robe off and making love to me on the floor?

Michael Oh, yes, that part quite definitely.

Joyce smiles and goes off

Michael sags, glancing across at George

Sorry.

George You learn new things all the time, don't you? If I'd had any idea that Joyce wanted to make love on the floor, well, of course, I'd have obliged like a shot.

Michael I don't think it was the floor *as such*.

George No?

Michael I think it was more the spontaneity of the idea that appealed.

George Oh. Spontaneity was never my strong suit.

Michael Be grateful. It's more trouble than it's worth.

There is a moment of companionable silence between them

George The coast's clear now, Mike. I don't think you should keep Debbie waiting any longer.

Michael No more sudden manifestations, George, all right?

George Whatever else happens tonight, you're on your own.

Michael Scouts honour?
George They threw me out of the Scouts after that tent-pitching débâcle.
   Will the Cubs do?
Michael They'll do fine.

George makes the Cubs salute. Michael smiles

   Goodnight, George.
George 'Night, Mike.

George goes off

*Michael quietly opens the door to the bedroom. The Lights cross-fade to
Debbie's room. Debbie is still angry with him but obviously relieved at his
return*

Debbie Well?
Michael I'm here, aren't I?
Debbie (*with difficulty*) If you knew how much this meant to me you'd
   understand why I have to be sure of you.

He squats down uneasily. She cuddles up against his back

Michael It's never easy picking up exactly where you left off, is it?
Debbie Maybe the best thing is to start all over again. (*She wraps her arms
   around him*)

*They kiss. He is finally beginning to get in the required mood when she breaks
away to look at him*

   I love you, Michael.

*Her sweet sincerity brings him up short. He looks into her eyes then holds her
out gently at arm's length*

Michael Debbie, maybe we should talk.
Debbie I don't want to talk. I want to make love.
Michael It's not that I don't want to … it's just that I don't think I can do it
   under false pretences.
Debbie What do you mean?
Michael I can honestly say this has never happened to me before.
Debbie Oh… If you just relax I'm sure it'll be all right.
Michael I'm talking about conscience, not impotence. Although it probably
   amounts to the same thing.

Debbie I don't understand.

Michael (*gently*) Debbie, I should think making love with you would be about as nice as the experience gets, and if all you wanted was a bit of fun then I'd be your man. But you want more than that because you love me.

Pause

And the truth is I don't think I love you.

Debbie (*angrily*) I knew it. All that stupid dog business——

He puts a finger on her lips

(*Tearfully*) You told me you did...

Michael I was lying. It was a ploy to get you into bed.

Debbie You don't love me at all, then?

Michael I love you a lot. But not enough.

Debbie Is it because you love Helen?

Michael (*after a moment*) No. I don't really love her, either.

Debbie I suppose it's hypocritical of me to say it, but she deserves better than that.

Michael I know she does.

Debbie (*struggling for calm*) Well. Thank you for telling me. It's turning out to be quite a day, isn't it?

Michael You'd be surprised.

The Lights dim on the extension, and come up on Joyce in the hall. George stands near her

Joyce Helen? Are you still awake?

Helen (*off*) What is it?

Joyce I wondered if you were all right in that bed?

Helen appears in her nightdress

Helen Of course I'm all right.

Joyce Oh.

Pause

Only, if you weren't, you could always share the big bed in my room. It's the strangest thing. I feel a bit lost in it. It seems to have got bigger overnight.

Helen You're imagining things.

Joyce (*sharply*) Of course I'm imagining things. I didn't seriously believe my bed was expanding.
Helen Yes, yes, all right.
Joyce Sorry.

Pause

You're probably all warm and comfy now anyway.
Helen No, not really. I can't seem to sleep either.
Joyce Then you wouldn't mind keeping me company?
Helen I'll get my gown.

The Lights go up in the bedroom. Michael is putting his clothes on

Michael I'd like it if we could still be friends, Debbie.
Debbie I was really hoping you'd have the originality not to use that line.
Michael Sorry. But if it makes it any better, I do mean it.
Debbie (*fiercely*) I don't know if I can forgive you yet. (*She pauses. More sadly*) Or stop loving you.
Michael I wouldn't have been any good for you, Debbie.

Pause

Friends? (*He holds out his hand*)

She looks at him ruefully but finally shakes on it

Now that we're clear about where we stand, I don't suppose there's any chance of a quick...

She glares at him

No ... probably not. (*He turns to go*)
Debbie Michael?
Michael Yes?
Debbie Thanks for being honest.
Michael I thought I'd try it sometime to see what it's like. But I'm not sure it's really me.
Debbie I think it suits you very well.

He crosses to the door, pausing briefly to talk under his breath

Michael Did I do the right thing, George?

Suddenly overcome by emotion, Debbie goes to him, hugging him and burying her head in his neck. He pats her softly, feeling smugly pleased with himself. Then he opens the door. The Lights go up in the hall, where Joyce and Helen stand next to each other and George stands watching placidly. They see Michael and Debbie in what looks like a fervent embrace. Michael's face falls with horror

Helen...! Joyce...! Still up, then?

Hold on them all for a split second, before the Lights go down

SCENE 3

A weary Michael stands with the phone to his ear

Michael Of course this isn't a bad moment, Lucille. Four o'clock is fine. I'm an early riser.
Lucille's Voice Well, that's good. I gotta tell you, I was kind of confused about what happened earlier.
Michael Just a misunderstanding. I fired my secretary the moment I heard about the mix-up.
Lucille's Voice That's nice.

Pause

OK, Mr Marlowe, here's the scoop. We like your project.
Michael Oh, thank God.
Lucille's Voice We just want a few minor changes before we show it to Mr Stallone...
Michael Oh, well, sure, I don't see that as a problem...
Lucille's Voice Firstly, we don't think it's appropriate for his character to die at the end.
Michael You don't?
Lucille's Voice We thought it would be kind of neat if he gets away after the execution.
Michael *(tactfully)* I don't think there's any real chance he would have survived a beheading, to be honest.
Lucille's Voice *(laughing)* I guess not, but wouldn't it be terrific if some faithful retainer took his place at the last second?
Michael *(stunned)* I don't know why I didn't think of that.
Lucille's Voice The servant takes his place on the block and Monmouth makes it to France. And then, and you'll love this, and then it's *Monmouth's son* who succeeds James to the throne of England!

There is a long silence as Michael struggles to compose his answer

Michael Strictly speaking, Lucille, and I'm afraid the history books are fairly
   firm on this point, it was William and Mary who succeeded James.
Lucille's Voice (*as though to an idiot*) Sure, and William the Orange was
   Monmouth's illegitimate son.
Michael It's not so much William *the* Orange, as William *of* Orange.
Lucille's Voice Whatever.
Michael One small problem... I think you'll find that William and
   Monmouth were roughly the same age...
Lucille's Voice Come on, Mr Marlowe, loosen up. This is the movies.
Michael (*heated*) This is not that kind of movie, Lucille. This picture has
   integrity. Your ideas would cheapen the whole meaning of it.

There is a long silence at the end of the line

   Lucille?
Lucille's Voice I'm sorry you feel that way, Mr Marlowe.
Michael It's not that I don't value your contribution——
Lucille's Voice If that's your final word——
Michael No, no, wait. Please. (*He pauses. Desperately*) Monmouth's
   bastard son William finally wins the throne ... it does have a ... pleasing
   irony...
Lucille's Voice (*alarmed*) Irony doesn't play in the Mid-West, Mr Marlowe.
Michael No, no, of course... I mean, there may be a pinch of irony in it, but
   so little they'd hardly notice... Lucille...

Pause

   Lucille, if I make these changes, will you show it to him?
Lucille's Voice He has a lot of other offers.
Michael But you'll give it serious consideration?
Lucille's Voice We'll get back to you. Goodnight, Mr Marlowe.
Michael (*passionately*) I'll make any changes you want if you'll just give
   me a break!

*There is only silence at the end of the line. The Lights go down on Michael's
bleak expression*

SCENE 4

The Lights go up on the living-room

Michael, Debbie and Helen are seated around the breakfast table in bitter silence. Michael is exiled to the end of the table. He looks exhausted and dejected

The only sound is the occasional scraping of toast

Michael (*eventually*) More tea?

Helen and Debbie look at him with contempt. He sighs and puts down the pot. Suddenly there is the sound of a revving car engine, rapidly followed by an awful wrenching and bending of metal on metal and the sound of repeated shunting and banging. Michael, Debbie and Helen look up in amazement. The sound continues for a few more seconds then stops abruptly

Silence

Joyce enters

Joyce I think you'll find that's the last time he'll park in front of *this* house. (*She sits down calmly*)

The others stare at her in amazement

Silence

Michael Look, about last night...

They look at him stonily. In despair, he tries adopting a more forceful approach

I wish you'd told me they'd rung, Joyce.

Joyce glares at him contemptuously

Helen Sylvester Stallone as the Duke of Monmouth. What can we expect from your next film, Michael? Richard The Third starring Flipper?
Michael Look, don't you think I know it's not ideal? Of course I'd like some brilliant young actor who nobody's ever heard of, but that's just not how things work in the film industry. Hollywood wants stars. The audience

wants stars. Nobody knows who I am and right now nobody cares, but if I can deliver a star they'll all sit up and pay attention. And then maybe *next time* I'll have enough power to do it exactly the way it should be.

Helen Well, if you hadn't been so absurdly secretive about it, we might have been better prepared. Though God only knows why a Hollywood star would waste his time with you.

Michael He's going to do it. Mark my words.

Helen Your capacity for self-delusion is one of the wonders of the age. There's something almost heroic about it.

Michael You can be as cynical as you like.

Helen I hardly think you're in a position to talk about cynicism. (*She pauses. She looks around the table*) I still can't quite believe what happened last night. I've come to expect moral vacuousness from the comatose bimbos you meet in your trendy watering holes, Michael, but I hoped for a little more from my own sisters.

Joyce We've said all there is to say on that subject.

Helen You have, you mean. *I'm* only just getting started. *Both* of you falling for this hypocritical, dishonest, disloyal, slimy ... *polecat*. It beggars the imagination.

Debbie You did the same thing once, Hel.

Helen At least I have the excuse that I didn't *know* he was a drunken apology for a human being.

Michael (*abjectly*) I'm sorry, Hel.

Helen (*dripping with sarcasm*) You've apologised. Oh well, that makes everything all right.

Joyce Oh, do shut up, Helen, you're giving me a headache.

Helen Any attempt to take the moral high-ground is going to look pretty dim coming from you, Joyce.

Joyce All I want to do is finish my breakfast in peace.

Helen Betrayed by my own sisters. I'm only glad George wasn't around to witness the whole pathetic episode.

Michael You'd be amazed.

Debbie Shut up, Michael.

Helen Didn't either of you think about me?

Debbie I'm truly sorry, Helen. It's just I've always had this crush on Michael and when he responded I ... lost my head.

Helen Well, that's something. Joyce?

Joyce I'd prefer not to talk about it.

Helen I suppose I can understand that you weren't yourself. By any standards yesterday wasn't a normal day.

Michael You can say that again.

Joyce Shut up, Michael.

Helen (*to Joyce*) But I do think some attempt to explain and make amends might be in order.

Joyce (*with dignity*) Debbie and I were clearly in the wrong. Whether you forgive us or not is entirely up to you. In your position I have no idea what I'd do.

Pause

But I can't help thinking that if there are hard words to be said some of them should be directed at the person mainly responsible for the trouble.

The sisters turn as one to look at Michael

Michael I preferred it when you were fighting among yourselves.

Helen The thing I'd really like to know, Michael, is whether you ever really loved me at all.

Michael Of course I did.

Helen For once I thought I'd found the right man; someone who wasn't gay, wasn't married and didn't take his washing home to his mother every Friday; finally, a man who didn't need me to dress up in a rubber diving suit before he could get sexually aroused——

Debbie I didn't know you'd done that.

Helen It's not the kind of thing that often comes up in conversation.

Debbie What was it like?

Helen At moments like that you come to realize that sex really isn't worth the bother.

Pause

Look, do you mind? I'm trying to say something to Michael.

Debbie Sorry.

Helen For once I'd got somebody normal. Except that you're not normal, are you, Michael? You're so chronically selfish, so completely terrified of any semblance of commitment, so utterly unable to cope with any trace of real emotion, that you have to ruin things the moment they show any sign at all of actually being worthwhile and lasting. (*She pauses*) And now I come to think about it, perhaps that means you are normal after all. Perhaps that's just the way men behave.

Joyce (*quietly*) Not all men.

The others turn to look at her, but she doesn't meet their gaze

Michael (*after a moment, to Helen*) Does this mean we're breaking up, then?

Helen I would rather be dipped head first in boiling oil than carry on going out with you for one second longer.

Michael I'll take that as a "yes".

Helen I don't want you coming back to the flat. You can send for your clothes when you've found somewhere else. (*She looks at her watch*) The markets are open.

Helen gets up and goes out

Debbie (*to Michael*) Where are you going to live now?

Michael Something will turn up, I expect.

Joyce picks up the dirty plates and goes out

Debbie pauses to look at the dejected Michael

Debbie I wish you'd told me. Helen I could cope with but Joyce as well...

Michael It was more of an accident than anything else.

Debbie Running someone over on a zebra crossing is an accident, Michael. I don't think taking women to bed falls into the same category.

Michael I didn't intend it to happen.

Debbie (*after a moment*) Why didn't you sleep with me when you had the chance?

Michael Because there's something about you that made me feel I had to behave myself for once.

Debbie There's nothing very special about me. After all I was prepared to deceive Helen, wasn't I? Don't put me up on a pedestal, Michael. I'm as fallible as the next person.

Michael As the next person at the moment is me, I rather doubt that.

Debbie But you did the right thing last night. By me, anyway.

Michael (*brightening*) I suppose I did, didn't I?

Pause

Debbie, as Helen and I aren't together now, what about you and me? I mean I'm sure, given time, I could grow to love you...

Debbie Sorry, Michael. I can't take the chance. I've wasted too many years on this fantasy of loving you. It's time to move on. I'm going to go out now and meet some wonderful man who'll fall head over heels for me, and marry me, and have children with me, and grow old with me. (*She pauses. Less bravely*) The only problem is it might take a little time because I always thought it was going to be you.

Michael I wish it could have been.

Debbie But one day soon I'll look at you and think to myself "What did I ever see in him?"

Pause

And when that happens, I know I'm ready for the real thing.

Michael (*wistfully*) Whoever you choose will be a lucky man, Debbie.

Debbie (*picking up the plates*) I'll get these out to Joyce, then I better go and pack.

Michael No hard feelings, then?

Debbie (*shaking her head*) I'm looking forward to seeing this film of yours.

Michael (*simply*) It might be a long wait. (*He pauses*) See you.

Debbie See you. (*She goes to the door*)

Michael Debbie? You chose the wrong brother. What you need is a man like George.

Debbie (*smiling*) That would be great. (*She pauses*) Only I wouldn't mind if he was a *bit* more handy around the house.

Debbie goes out

Michael slumps down in his chair

George enters, dressed as before

George That was a very nice thing to say, Mike.

Michael Think nothing of it.

George I can see this practical thing really is pretty important to women. When I come back it's going to be as a handyman or plumber or something.

Michael Ah-ha.

George Ah-ha? What do you mean, "Ah-ha"?

Michael So it's reincarnation, is it?

George Did I say that?

Michael You certainly did. You said "When I come back".

George Oh, that was just a figure of speech.

Michael (*disappointed*) So it's not reincarnation?

George It *might* be.

Michael If you're going to tease me I'll pretend you're not here.

George I told you, I'm really not allowed to say. It's a bit like the Mafia. There's nothing actually stopping you from talking, but there's hell to pay if you do. (*He pauses*) Anyway, reincarnation might not be such good news in your case. On present form you're liable to come back as a cockroach.

Michael looks down glumly

Oh, come on, Mike. You have to see the funny side of it all.

Michael stares at him balefully

Look, if it makes you feel any better, you're not the only one in hot water. That interfering rule was stricter than I thought.

Michael (*after a moment*) I've worked out your mission, George. You came back to stop me ruining Debbie's life.

George Oh, that's what you think?

Michael It's pretty obvious, isn't it?

George (*giving nothing away*) You always were a clever one, Mike.

Michael And thank God you did. The fact that I didn't break her heart is about the only good thing to come out of this whole gruesome episode.

George You haven't considered another possibility? That you might have behaved the way you did because of the way *you* felt. Don't you think that if the will had been there to do it, nothing I said would have made the slightest difference?

Michael (*laughing*) You mean it was my own conscience stopping me?

George Why not?

Michael It's a nice idea, George. But it's not very convincing, is it?

George Isn't it?

Michael I'm incapable of that level of nobility under my own steam.

George I think you're underestimating yourself.

Michael Look, I know you're trying to make me feel better. But we both know the truth. I'm just not a very worthwhile person. (*He tries to rally, with unconvincing cheerfulness*) You know, George, I'm getting to like the idea of having you perched on my shoulder like some kind of superannuated Jiminy Crickit. I think we're going to have to agree a few ground rules, though——

George (*cutting in*) You're forgetting something, Mike. I'm only here for a day or two. (*He pauses*) In fact, I only dropped by now to say farewell.

Michael (*dismayed*) You're going?

George Oh, yes.

Michael How long for?

George Eternity, I suppose. I did tell you.

Michael Yes, I know. It's a shock, that's all. I'd just got used to having you around again.

George Well, *assuming* your theory is correct, now that Debbie's safe, there's nothing else for me to do here, is there?

Michael I suppose not.

George (*slyly*) I mean, the only point in my staying around now would be *if there was something else I could do for the family*. Right?

Michael Right.

George So, *if there isn't*, it must be time for me to go.

Michael fails to pick up on George's enigmatic tone

Michael I'll miss you.

George And I you.

Michael There's no chance you might pop in from time to time?

George It's the people who hang around for centuries that give ghosts a bad name.

Michael This is it, then?

George This is it.

Michael No last-minute homilies?

George No.

Michael (*very upset*) Take care, won't you?

George You bet. You too. Bye then.

Michael George——

Although George still stands where he was, Michael can no longer see him

George? (*He pauses. Helplessly*) What am I supposed to do now?

George smiles kindly

Michael waits, then goes out

Joyce enters

She goes to wipe the breakfast table. George watches her affectionately. After a moment she begins to slow down until finally she stops altogether and stands staring out, lost in thought

Joyce (*after a moment*) Are you there, George?

George Joyce?

Joyce (*not hearing him*) I expect you were pretty unimpressed by last night's performance. Not really the kind of thing you'd expect from me, is it? Well, I'm not going to apologise...

George You don't have to...

Joyce Don't be shocked, George, but I'd been thinking about him ever since you died. Looking at it now, I wonder if it isn't what got me through the whole terrible week. As long as Michael was taking up space in my thoughts I could keep on pushing you to one side. And you know the really odd thing? If you hadn't died, I'm pretty sure I wouldn't even have given him a second thought. The whole silly, drunken episode would have been forgotten about. What sense does that make? Odd, aren't they, the things we do to survive a crisis. (*She pauses*) You know, I'm still furious with you.

George (*softly*) That's reassuring.

Joyce What were you thinking about, going and leaving me like this? I married you because you were safe and reliable. I thought I could *depend* on you. (*She pauses*) Safe and reliable. Not the most romantic qualities, are they? In the beginning I was looking for someone with a bit more mystery to them; the risky, unpredictable men were the ones I liked. But for some reason they never came my way. Perhaps I scared them all off. And then one day I realized that there was a very real possibility I might end up on my own. And I couldn't face that. I couldn't bear to be lonely. So I took you; kind, patient, ponderous, good-humoured old George. (*She pauses*) And I never quite forgave you for just being you.

George looks at her sadly but without reproach

I know you loved me, George. I don't know how I became this bad-tempered, bossy seaside postcard of a wife. I married you knowing full well what you were and then I tried to change you. Of course, that was bound to fail and the more obvious the failure the more angry I became. Why do we do that to people? Why can't we just let them be what they are? (*She pauses*) I know it's too late to say it, George, but I'm sorry if I made your life a misery.

George You never did that, Joyce. Not for a minute.

Joyce I should have faced up to my own fears and insecurities all those years ago and just let you go on your own sweet way. (*She pauses*) It would have been better for you if we'd never clapped eyes on each other.

George (*very moved*) I wish you could hear me, Joyce. I wish you could understand that I wouldn't have missed our life together for anything.

Joyce But I will miss you, George. I do already. I've been numb for a week, but this morning I felt a dull ache in my stomach, so I think it must be starting. I'm glad it's there at last. I was beginning to think it would never come. And I would have hated myself if it hadn't. (*She pauses and smiles*) Listen to me talking to myself. That's something I never did before, isn't it? Although, let's face it, sometimes when you were here it *felt* as though I was, for all the answer I got. (*She pauses*) Perhaps I'll turn into one of those cranky old eccentrics, nattering to myself at bus stops.

George Somehow I don't think so. Not really your style.

Joyce Somehow I don't think so. Not really my style.

George smiles at the coincidence

I'll take a deep breath, pin my shoulders back, and wait to see what turns up next. (*She pauses. Less certainly*) I just wish I could think what on earth it might be.

George You'll know when you find it. I promise you.

Joyce Goodbye, George.

George Good luck, Joycie.

Joyce (*pausing at the door*) Oh, and George?
George (*forgetting she can't hear him*) Yes?
Joyce Wherever you are now, I hope they have an enormous library.

Joyce goes out

George pauses wistfully, then follows her

Michael comes in with a magazine

He tries to read but has no real interest in it

He looks up as Helen enters, barking into her mobile

Helen …Right … right … OK. I'll be with you in an hour. Don't do a *thing* until I get there. (*She snaps the mouthpiece closed*) You'd never believe it. The yen's just disappeared over the horizon dragging the euro in it's wake. I have to get back to sort it out.
Michael Don't be too hard on them. They're young irresponsible currencies but they mean well.
Helen (*smiling*) In a way I suppose I should thank you, Michael.
Michael I'm sure you're right, but just at this precise moment I can't imagine why.
Helen You've made me realize I was crazy to feel guilty about loving work more than you.
Michael I think deep down I always knew I was second best, Hel.
Helen No man has ever given me the satisfaction my job does. I used to think there was something wrong with that, but now I'm not so sure. Why not just accept that studying the FTSE share price index gets me more excited than a romantic date? Why worry that a fall in the Bundesbank interest rate is sexier than having someone whispering sweet nothings in my ear? (*She pauses*) The fact is, Michael, that even when we were making love my mind was more likely to be on stocks and shares than it was on you.
Michael I wondered why you sometimes yelled "Sell, Sell!" at the crucial moment.
Helen (*smiling*) I've never felt lonely on my own. Why should I feel bad about that? Why rush headlong into another messy relationship just because it's supposed to make me feel complete?
Michael They don't have to be messy.
Helen I hope you're right. I really do. But until the day comes when a man does for me what the markets can, I'm finished with them. I'm staying faithful to Lloyds of London for now.
Michael I hope you'll be very happy together.

Helen (*with unexpected tenderness*) Try not to make a total mess of everything. (*She kisses him on the cheek*)

Helen goes off

Michael is left a dejected and lonely figure. He sits on the sofa

George enters and sits next to him

Joyce enters

Michael Everyone's gone.

Joyce Except you.

Michael I'm just gathering strength.

Joyce Shouldn't you be off bringing Hollywood to its knees?

Michael I can't seem to get kick-started, somehow. I'm incredibly tired.

Joyce After your priapic marathon last night, I'm not surprised.

Michael Are you still angry with me?

Joyce Not really.

Michael (*astounded*) No?

Joyce Don't try the little boy lost act on me. I'm not in the mood.

Michael That just about exhausts my repertoire, then.

Joyce Self-pitying claptrap. You have a great many attributes.

Michael Maybe. But film producing isn't one of them.

Joyce I thought you said it was all set? I thought your actor was all lined up and the financiers raring to go?

Michael That wasn't strictly true.

Joyce Which part?

Michael All of it really. An actor like Sylvester Stallone isn't going to bother with losers like me. Helen was right. It's all just a self-deluding fantasy.

Joyce This isn't like you, Michael.

Michael I'm a joke. I can talk the talk, but when it comes to closing a deal I'm hopeless. One look at the real players and my insides turn to liquid. They could cut me into strips and use me for dental floss, and they know it.

Joyce Well, you'll simply have to toughen up.

Michael I've tried that. It was about as convincing as Clint Eastwood in a dress.

Joyce What about this script of yours. Is it any good?

Michael Oh, yes, it's not bad. I can manage that bit. But there are lots of people out there with decent projects. The trick is persuading the money men to take a chance on you.

Joyce You always sounded convincing to me.

Michael You and George wanted to believe in me. The people with the money don't. They've got built-in crap-detectors that go off the minute I walk into the room. (*He pauses*) I just have to face the fact that I don't have what it takes. From tomorrow I'm going to stop pretending and start looking for another job.

Joyce I see.

Michael I'm a failure, pure and simple. More so than George ever was.

George smiles

Joyce I've never thought of you as a failure.

Michael Well, it's about time you did. (*He pauses*) Tomorrow is the first day of the rest of my life.

Joyce You're not going to sing, are you? That sounded like the cue for an orchestra.

Michael (*smiling*) I don't know what's wrong with me. I had an attack of conscience last night and today I'm facing the truth about my life. I wonder if I'm ill?

Joyce Growing up, possibly.

Michael Ouch. I suppose I deserved that. (*He pauses*) It's going to be strange without George around, isn't it?

Joyce (*awkwardly*) Yes.

Michael Things are all right about him, you know.

Joyce What do you mean?

George leans forward, interested in Michael's response

Michael I just know that somehow or other ... he's OK.

Joyce Are you feeling all right, Michael?

Michael It's a bit difficult to explain. All I mean is that you don't have to worry about him. (*He gathers himself*) I suppose I ought to be moving along.

Joyce looks at him thoughtfully. Michael gets up and walks to the door. George looks to Joyce in alarm

George Go on, Joycie. Say it. You know you want to.

Joyce (*after a moment*) There's no rush, Michael.

George looks relieved

Michael I've already been an embarrassment to you, Joyce. I don't want to be a burden as well.

Joyce Stop being so nauseatingly humble.

Michael Sorry.

Joyce And stop saying "sorry". If you keep on apologising all the time it's no wonder you don't impress the moguls. They interpret it as weakness.

Michael You're probably right, but you know, I just don't think I care any more. I've had it. I'm finished with the whole game. (*He pauses*) Look, I better get going.

Joyce Where to?

Michael I haven't the faintest idea.

Joyce You've got nowhere to sleep.

Michael I'll be all right on a park bench. Don't worry about me.

Joyce Wait a minute.

Pause

Look, you can stay here for a few days while you get yourself sorted out.

George grins in satisfaction

Michael Well...

Joyce All I ask in return is that you do a few jobs around the house. You can start with the fence.

Michael hesitates, then shrugs his agreement

The Lights go down, then up on George watching as Michael paints the fence. Bird song in the background. Joyce watches the work carefully. The fence is nearly finished. It shines

You don't think matt might have been more hard-wearing?

Michael (*smiling*) Probably, but I just had this overwhelming feeling that gloss was the thing for this job. We want to make an impression, don't we?

Joyce We certainly do. (*She pauses. Chattily*) It must be pretty hard getting hold of these top Hollywood people then?

Michael (*concentrating on the painting*) Not necessarily.

Joyce I thought you said they were too grand to deal with the small fry?

Michael Yes, but they have to be careful. After all, no-one wants to miss out on the next big thing. It's just a question of convincing them you've got something worthwhile.

Joyce (*thoughtfully*) I see. (*She pauses*) Don't forget to clean up the front lawn when you've finished, will you?

The Lights go down, then up on Michael who now has a rake in his hand. Again Joyce is supervising keenly, while George is the same silent presence. Michael's rucksack is on the floor at his feet

(*Pointing*) Don't forget the weeding.

Michael (*long-suffering*) I'll get to it in a minute.

Joyce (*smiling*) I bet you're wishing you hadn't given up the film industry, after all.

Michael Not me.

Joyce It's a pity you couldn't make your film the way you originally wanted to.

Michael Without stars, you mean? Maybe I could have done. I just couldn't make anyone believe in me.

Joyce Surely it's not that simple?

Michael You'd be surprised. It's a bit like selling insurance. If you believe in yourself enough you can convince anybody of anything. (*He pauses*) Can I have a cup of tea, Joyce? I'm gasping.

Joyce You can have tea when you're finished. (*She pauses*) Well, all right, then. The tea's in the cupboard over the sink. White, no sugar for me.

Michael rolls his eyes. Joyce smiles

Michael I should have taken that park bench when I had the chance.

Michael goes off

Joyce quickly goes over to his rucksack and rummages through it until she finds the script of Rebellion!. *She half takes it out, but then pauses guiltily. George rolls his eyes in frustration*

George Go on. What are you waiting for?

Joyce finally shrugs as though to suggest the whole idea is stupid and replaces the script in the bag. She gets up and walks away, her back to George. George shakes his head, then picks up the bag himself, glancing up to the skies apologetically

Just this once. I promise. (*He takes out the script and tosses it on the ground at Joyce's feet*)

She turns, gazing at it in astonishment. She looks around in confusion but can find no explanation. She is about to put the script back in the bag but this time curiosity gets the better of her. She glances at the first page, then, with a last puzzled look, tucks it eagerly under her arm

Joyce goes off

George smiles in satisfaction

The Lights go down, then up on Michael, who is crouched painting something that we can't yet see. Joyce watches him intently

George still hovers nearby

Michael Producing films is like playing poker. It's mostly a question of bluffing with confidence.
Joyce You manage that with women well enough.

Michael smiles good-humouredly. There is a growing warmth between them

But there must be lots of technical and legal aspects to it?
Michael Oh, you can always hire people to handle the details. The producer is more like a ringmaster, pulling everything together.
Joyce Surely you can't just wander in and do it without any training?
Michael All that matters is having enough belief in yourself. (*He glances up ruefully, then shrugs off the subject and looks back proudly at his handiwork*) What do you think? (*He stands up to reveal two traffic cones sandwiching a sign announcing in bold capitals "Absolutely No Parking At Any Time"*)

Joyce looks at it with satisfaction

Joyce Perfect.

They smile at each other, then look away, embarrassed by an unexpected intimacy

As Michael and Joyce go off, George moves to the front of the stage, relaxed and at peace with himself. He smiles, then exits

The Lights go up on the living-room where Joyce sits on the sofa

She clicks off the phone as Michael appears in the doorway, looking bleary in open-necked shirt and jeans

Good morning, Michael.
Michael (*sleepily*) Please don't make me work yet, Joyce. I'm shattered.
Joyce You've been asleep for twelve hours.
Michael My God. Somebody must have sprinkled fairy dust on me.
Joyce I imagine it makes a change from the stuff you're used to inhaling. Now wake up and pay attention. I want to talk to you. (*She pauses*) I've read your script.

Michael Have you? Why?

Joyce (*ignoring him*) It could be improved in a number of areas but it's not bad.

Michael Thank you very——

Joyce I haven't finished yet. After I'd read it I began to think there might be something I could do about it. After all, I do have a talent for organisation.

Michael I don't quite see what you're driving at, Joyce——

Joyce If you stopped interrupting you might find out. Now, I have to confess to taking a liberty. While you were asleep I went through your bag and found your address book.

Michael Why?

Joyce Because Sylvester Stallone wasn't listed in the Yellow Pages under "Actors".

Michael But why did you want his number?

Joyce (*as though to a child*) Because I thought he could help us make the film. (*She pauses*) His people really do like the project, you know.

Michael You *spoke* to them?

Joyce They'd somehow got hold of this odd idea that William of Orange was Monmouth's illegitimate son, but once I'd set them straight on that things went remarkably smoothly.

Michael (*wildly excited*) You mean he's going to do it?

Joyce No, of course not. You didn't really want him playing Monmouth, did you?

Michael (*deflated*) Didn't I?

Joyce You know you didn't. Anyone could see he's not right for it. But a nice girl called Louise gave me some numbers to call and I found another company who seemed very keen. They said England is very fashionable at the moment and they want to spend their money here. They've read the script and they're willing to put up the cash.

Michael (*stunned*) With no strings attached?

Joyce I told them we wanted a talented unknown to play the lead role and they're willing to back our judgement.

Michael I don't believe it.

Joyce I agreed to let them be something called "Executive Producers". Was that all right?

Michael (*weakly*) Fine.

Joyce (*with relish*) I made them sweat a bit on that, though. I didn't think it would be a good idea to look too keen.

Michael (*awed*) Joyce, are you telling me you've set up the film?

Joyce Well, not quite, perhaps. But I think I can safely say we're on the way.

Michael (*going to hug her*) You're an absolute miracle worker...!

Joyce Don't do that. I've only just put my make-up on.

Michael This calls for a drink. (*He goes to the cabinet and takes out the whisky*)

Joyce gazes at him beadily. He hesitates under her withering scrutiny, glances wistfully at the bottle, then finally screws the top back on with an air of determination. She nods approvingly. Michael shakes his head in wonder

I don't understand how you did it.

Joyce Oh, it's quite fun once you get into the swing of it. Which leads me to my next point. I've been thinking about what I'm going to do without George. I certainly don't intend to stay at home vegetating. Looking back, I think that was my problem all along. I needed something to do. So, here's what I propose. You have charm and a reasonable eye for talent, but all the business instincts of a gerbil. I, on the other hand have very little interest in the creative side, but seem to have a knack for the sharp end. In my book that sounds like a perfect match. I think you and I should go into partnership together. Is that acceptable?

Michael I... I ... don't see why not.

Joyce Unless of course you're still determined to give the whole business up?

Michael (*after a long moment*) You've saved my life, Joyce.

Joyce (*quietly*) Perhaps we both needed a little saving.

Michael I could kiss you.

Joyce That brings us to another point entirely. Obviously it's going to be more convenient if you stay here for the time being. My proposal is that in return for board and lodging you keep the house in good repair. Of course, when any revenue comes into the company we'll split it fifty-fifty. (*She pauses*) But this is a purely business relationship and I expect you to treat it as such. Kissing is out of the question. Is that clearly understood?

Michael Perfectly.

Joyce (*more softly*) Of course, all company regulations are eligible for review on a continuing basis.

Michael smiles. Joyce blushes and looks away

Well. I think that covers everything.

Michael Sounds like it.

Joyce Now, if we're going to be partners the first thing you'll have to do is smarten yourself up. Part of your problem is presentation. You need to be taken in hand. (*She pauses*) And if you attempt to extract any kind of smutty innuendo from that last sentence our partnership is over.

Michael grins at her then bounces cheerfully out of the room

Joyce smiles to herself then stands up. She is just about to leave when something catches her eye tucked almost out of sight under the cushion of the armchair. She pulls it out. It is a tie. To be precise, the same striking tie that

George was buried in and has been wearing throughout. She looks at it in
bewilderment

That's odd… What's this doing here? I could have sworn… (*She stares at*
the tie, knowing it should be with George in his coffin. In bewilderment)
George? (*After a moment she shrugs and smiles to herself, looking at the*
tie in approval) Very smart, though I say it myself. (*She calls*) Michael?
Michael! I've got something for you. I think it'll suit you perfectly.

Joyce exits, carrying the tie in triumph

CURTAIN

FURNITURE AND PROPERTY LIST

Further dressing may be added at the director's discretion

ACT I

SCENE 1

On stage: 2 lived-in armchairs with cushions
Mismatched office sofa with cushions
Dining table
Drinks cabinet. *In it*: crisps, bottles of drinks including whisky and gin
Glasses
Coffee table
Fireplace
Cordless phone
Net curtains on windows
Picture of **George** and **Joyce** on wall
Light switch on wall

Off stage: 2 dessert bowls with jelly, 2 spoons (**Debbie**)
Tray with tea things (**Joyce**)

Personal: **Helen:** mobile phone

SCENE 2

Strike: Tray with tea things

Off stage: Newspaper (**George**)
Bottle of champagne, tatty-looking bunch of flowers (**Michael**)
Michael's flowers in small vase, ice bucket (**Joyce**)
Towel, hairdryer (**Joyce**)

SCENE 3

Strike: Newspaper
Bottle of champagne

Vase with flowers
Ice bucket

ACT II

Scene 1

On stage: As before

Personal: **Helen:** cigarettes, lighter
Joyce: kitchen knife

Scene 2

On stage: Rickety-looking camp bed with bedclothes
Magazine

Scene 3

On stage: As Act I, Scene 1

Scene 4

Set: Breakfast things: pieces of toast on plates, pot of tea, cups, etc.

Off stage: Kitchen towel (**Joyce**)
Magazine (**Michael**)

Personal: **Helen:** watch, mobile phone

During Black-out on page 74:

Set: Paint
Brush
Shiny fence, nearly finished

Strike: Breakfast things
Magazine

During Black-out on page 74:

Set: Rake
Michael's rucksack containing script of *Rebellion!*

Strike: Paint
            Brush

During Black-out on page 75:

Set: 2 traffic cones with sign in bold capitals "Absolutely No Parking At
                Any Time"
            Paint
            Brush
            George's tie under cushion of armchair

Strike: Rake
            Michael's rucksack

LIGHTING PLOT

Property fittings required: nil
Various interior and exterior settings

ACT I, Prologue

To open: Slowly bring up spotlight on **George**

No cues

ACT I, Scene 1

To open: Evening lighting on living-room

Cue 1	**Michael** goes out *Cross-fade to hall*	(Page 13)
Cue 2	**Michael** reacts as **Debbie** nods *Cross-fade to living-room*	(Page 16)
Cue 3	**Michael** replenishes his glass *Gradually increase lights to unnatural brightness*	(Page 19)
Cue 4	**Michael** jiggles light switch up and down *After a moment, bring up lights to peak of intensity,* *then black-out*	(Page 19)
Cue 5	**Michael**: "Who said that?" *Bring up lighting; after a pause, black-out*	(Page 19)

ACT I, Scene 2

To open: Spotlight on **George**

Cue 6	**George**: "…I suppose I did." *Cross-fade to evening sunshine outside living-room*	(Page 19)
Cue 7	**George**: "…lift off!" *Flash and black-out*	(Page 35)

ACT I, SCENE 3

To open: Spotlight on **George**

Cue 8   **George**: "…willing to let me have a go."   (Page 36)
               Cross-fade to living-room

Cue 9   **Michael**: "George——"   (Page 43)
               Fade lights down

Cue 10   **George** exits   (Page 43)
               Bring up lights

Cue 11   **Michael** turns lights off and on   (Page 43)
               Snap lights off and on

Cue 12   **Michael** waits with his hand on the doorknob   (Page 43)
               After a moment, fade lights down

ACT II, SCENE 1

To open: Lighting on **Michael**

Cue 13   **Helen** lights a cigarette   (Page 45)
               *After a moment, black-out; then bring up lights
                  on* **George**

ACT II, SCENE 2

To open: Cross-fade to lighting on **Michael**

Cue 14   **Michael**: "Debbie?"   (Page 47)
               Bring up lights on **Debbie**'s room

Cue 15   **Michael** and **George** exit into hall   (Page 50)
               Cross-fade to hall

Cue 16   **Michael** rushes into **Debbie**'s room   (Page 52)
               Cross-fade to **Debbie**'s room

Cue 17   **Debbie**: "…unless you know what you really want." (Page 54)
               Cross-fade to hall

Cue 18	**Michael** opens door to **Debbie**'s room *Cross-fade to* **Debbie**'s room	(Page 58)
Cue 19	**Michael**: "You'd be surprised." *Fade lights down on* **Debbie**'s room, bring up lights on **Joyce** in hall	(Page 59)
Cue 20	**Helen**: "I'll get my gown." *Cross-fade to* **Debbie**'s room	(Page 60)
Cue 21	**Michael** opens door *Bring up lights on hall*	(Page 61)
Cue 22	**Michael**: "Still up, then?" *After a short pause, fade lights down*	(Page 61)

ACT II, SCENE 3

To open:	Night-time lighting on living-room	
Cue 23	**Michael**: "…just give me a break!" *After a pause, fade lights down*	(Page 62)

ACT II, SCENE 4

To open:	General lighting on living-room	
Cue 24	**Michael** shrugs his agreement *Fade lights down, then up when ready*	(Page 74)
Cue 25	**Joyce**: "…when you've finished, will you?" *Fade lights down, then up when ready*	(Page 74)
Cue 26	**George** smiles in satisfaction *Fade lights down, then up when ready*	(Page 75)
Cue 27	**George** exits *Bring up lights on living-room*	(Page 76)

EFFECTS PLOT

ACT I

Cue 1   To open Prologue   (Page 1)
Sombre music

Cue 2   Spotlight comes up on **George**   (Page 1)
Cut music

Cue 3   To open Act I, Scene 1   (Page 1)
Phone ringing tone

Cue 4   **Michael**: "I love you."   (Page 15)
After a pause, phone rings, off

Cue 5   **Joyce**: "Fine."   (Page 17)
Phone rings

Cue 6   **Joyce** watches through window   (Page 23)
Sound of car engines off, then sudden squealing of brakes

Cue 7   **George**: "…lift off!"   (Page 35)
Enormous bang followed by electric buzz

ACT II

Cue 8   Lights come up on **Michael**   (Page 44)
Nerve-tingling music, creating rising tension

Cue 9   **Michael**: "Joyce! No…"   (Page 44)
Music reaches frantic climax

Cue 10   **Michael** sighs and puts down the pot   (Page 63)
*Sound of revving car engine, rapidly followed by sound
of awful wrenching and bending of metal on metal and
repeated shunting and banging; continue for a few
seconds, then cut*

Cue 11   Lights come up on **Michael** painting fence (Page 74)
Bird song in background

www.ingramcontent.com/pod-product-compliance
Lightning Source LLC
LaVergne TN
LVHW051753080426
835511LV00018B/3312